S0-ALB-063

99 Jumpstarts to Research

99 Jumpstarts
to Research

Topic Guides for Finding Information on Current Issues

Peggy Whitley
Catherine Olson
Susan Williams Goodwin

2001

Libraries Unlimited
A Member of Greenwood Publishing Group, Inc.
88 Post Road West
Westport, CT 06881

CHABOT COLLEGE LIBRARY

ZA
3050
.W49
2001

Copyright © 2001 Libraries Unlimited
All Rights Reserved
Printed in the United States of America

No part of this publication may be reproduced, stored in a re-
trieval system, or transmitted, in any form or by any means,
electronic, mechanical, photocopying, recording, or otherwise,
without the prior written permission of the publisher.

LIBRARIES UNLIMITED
A Member of Greenwood Publishing Group, Inc.
88 Post Road West
Westport, CT 06881
1-800-237-6124
www.lu.com

Library of Congress Cataloging-in-Publication Data

Whitley, Peggy.
    99 jumpstarts to research : topic guides for finding information on current issues /
Peggy Whitley, Catherine Olson, Susan Williams Goodwin.
        p. cm.
    Includes bibliographical references and index.
    ISBN 1-56308-915-7
        1. Information resources--United States--Directories. 2. Research--United States. 3.
Report writing. I. Title: Ninety-nine jumpstarts to research. II. Olson, Catherine. III.
Goodwin, Susan Williams. IV. Title.

ZA3050 .W47 2001
025.5'24--dc21

                                                2001038276

Contents

Introduction

99 Jumpstarts to Research, created by three reference librarians, attempts to teach the beginning researcher good research habits. It provides names of tools students should consult for a well-rounded, well-researched paper on a controversial issue in the news. Books, specialized databases, online resources, and agencies to contact are all included. Although the book does not give users resources on a platter, it does "jumpstart" exploration into a topic. It is intended to help students "think through" a topic and the research process. *99 Jumpstarts to Research* teaches research methods through application.

Each jumpstart has been student tested at Kingwood College Library. The current topics used were chosen for their wide appeal, permanence, and controversy. Although classic topics such as abortion and animal research are included, a diverse variety of others may also be found, including welfare reform, school choice, lifetime benefits of sports, and the greenhouse effect. Students researching topics for psychology, sociology, English, government, or economics classes have found these jumpstarts useful. Teachers report that the use of these aids helps students become thorough researchers. Librarians have noticed that students return to the library as independent and informed users.

It is our hope that this book will help students, teachers, and librarians in other schools and colleges. We would like to give special thanks to other Kingwood College librarians who helped with this project, especially Bettye Sutton and Becky Bradley.

How This Book Is Organized

Each jumpstart is divided into the following sections:

- **Search Terms**: subject headings and keywords that can be used for searching the library catalog, periodical indexes, and the Internet.

- **Food for Thought**: definitions and explanations of and questions about a topic, suggesting various avenues for the researcher to explore.

- **Background and Statistics**: suggested relevant reference books to aid the user in gathering basic information. Note that a complete bibliography of all titles mentioned in this section is located at the back of this volume.

- **The Library Catalog**: a list of specific Library of Congress and Sears subject headings students can use in searching the catalog.

⊿ **Magazines and Newspapers**: a suggested list of periodical and newspaper indexes that students can consult. There may be other databases that we have not listed that would be appropriate. Check your local library to see what is available.

⊿ **Internet**: specific Internet addresses and suggested ways to find more Web sites using search engines. Authoritative Web sites have been selected that may not be found in a general keyword search.

⊿ **Agencies to Contact**: names, addresses, and phone numbers of government agencies, private organizations, and foundations that may be helpful.

Jumpstarts for Searching the World Wide Web

Both the experienced and the novice Web user can find help in this section. Take a few minutes to read through these pages. New and improved methods for using the Web are continuously being developed. Watch for them online.

Time-Saving Tips

1. Use search engine help commands. The Web changes faster than the rules or tips can be written.

2. Skip http://. It is no longer needed. Just type the URL; for example, www.whitehouse.gov

3. If you search a .com site using Netscape or Internet Explorer, you need only enter the name of the company; for example, Compaq, in the location line. You will automatically link to www.compaq.com

4. When returning to a previously visited site, use the right mouse button over the Back icon. You will be able to slide down the mouse arrow to any of the last 10 or so sites you have visited. Click and go directly to where you want to be.

5. When searching, the more specific your search terms, the more likely you will get what you want. You might even describe your search; for example, *need community college distance learning retention statistics.*

6. Use more than one search engine and use the power search or advanced search screens.

7. Directories, such as Yahoo, Lycos, and Netscape Search, are built by humans. They search for Web *sites* first, then Web *pages*. If you want an entire site, like a college or an association, use a directory.

8. Guess the URL; for example, www.utexas.edu. More often than not, you will be right. Companies, organizations, and colleges like to use an easy to guess URL.

9. Using the hints in "Where Do I Begin," select the type of search engine that is most appropriate for your search.

10. Select the best source for your information. For most students, online full-text databases are available in the library. We have listed these in the bibliography. Check with your librarian to see what your local library has available.

Where Do I Begin? What Type of Search Engine Do I Need?

Determine which of these four scenarios matches your search problem. Be sure to include hints from the timesaving tips and search techniques previously listed.

CASE STUDY 1

I know the results from this search will be HUGE! I just want to find the best sites without being inundated with too much information.

Consider using a metasearch database like Metacrawler (www.metacrawler.com). These engines search several databases at once and give only a few of the top-ranked sites. Select the *phrase* or *all these words* option. If you are using a different search engine, use the *Power* or *Advanced Searches* for limiting. Many databases now allow the user to narrow a large search by searching only the results list. Another excellent method of limiting is to search words you would like to see in the document title, like this: *title:student retention*. Several engines, such as Excite, HotBot, and Lycos, rank sites by how many other sites on the Internet link to it (popularity). There is a reason so many people link to a particular site.

CASE STUDY 2

I've looked and looked for this information. There just isn't much on my subject.

Use Alta Vista (www.altavista.com) or one of the other huge databases. Alta Vista and certain others search every word in a document. Type in as many search terms as you can, listing the most important words first, for example: *tuberculosis AIDS children treatment rejection "New York City"*.

Generally speaking, Google, Lycos, and Northern Light will find sites containing ALL of your terms. Alta Vista, Snap, Infoseek, and Yahoo will search for ANY of your search terms. To go deeper into a search, you may want to use *Use the Related Sites* or *More from this Site* features. Keep in mind that many search engines have databases of terms and phrases. Let them help you. Then, if you still do not find anything, consider going to an online specialized database.

If we were looking for the information in *tuberculosis AIDS children treatment rejection "New York City"*, we would go to an online searchable database such as MEDLINE or find an organization containing searchable fact sheets and essays, such as the Centers for Disease Control (CDC).

CASE STUDY 3

I am clueless. I don't know where to start. I am a rank beginner, or I have never searched for this kind of information. Help!

Try either of these two options. First, use AskJeeves (www.askjeeves.com) or another natural language engine. Northern Light is our favorite (www.northernlight.com). Type your question as though you are asking a librarian; for example, "Where will I find information containing statistics on student retention at the community college?" Jeeves organizes answers in an easy-to-view, scroll-less way. Many essays and articles are included.

Second, and probably more appropriately, use one of the better, more academic subject directory collections. Subject directories arrange information by subject, then sub-subject, then sub-sub-subject. The best directories tend to collect large searchable sites that you would not ordinarily know about or find in a normal search. Following are some recommendations:

- Yahoo (www.yahoo.com) is the mother of all subject directories. Yahoo accepts only the very best sites and has strong academic subject areas. The humans there collect Web sites, not Web pages.

- Direct Search (gwis2circ.gwu.edu/~gprice/direct.htm) is a library favorite. From George Washington University, Direct Search lists scholarly sites containing data not easily or entirely searchable or accessible using general search tools like Alta Vista, Google, or Infoseek.

- Internets has an enormous collection of subject searches and online databases at www.Internets.com/index.htm. Considered scholarly, Internets is better on some topics than others. It is certainly worth a try for your subjects.

- About.com is unique in that there are specialists in each subfield who find Web links, answer questions; offer chats; list related forums, events, conventions; and write newsletters on each subject at about.com. This is awesome in some categories. Check it out.

CASE STUDY 4

I've looked all over the Web. I'm ready to give up! What more can I do?

Consider a specialized database, such as ERIC for educational research or MEDLINE for the sciences. Many government, business, and medical databases are searchable online. Do not forget helpful online searchable newspapers or books, such as the *World Almanac* or *Occupational Outlook*. Many specialized databases and books will be found in the subject directory collections listed above. Academic libraries create subject guides linking to the most important databases and Web sites on a topic. Usually the librarians know sites you would not find in a standard search. Subject guides at the authors' library at Kingwood College are available for everyone and located online at www.nhmccd.edu/lrc/kc/subjects.html. Another old and well-respected collection of subject guides is Argus Clearinghouse, www.clearinghouse.com.

Search Techniques for the Web

Type of Search	Example	Description
Title word search	Title:assisted suicide	Results contain search words in the title (above the line) of a Web page, e.g., a search including title:assisted suicide would find pages with that phrase in the title. This is a valuable technique but is dependent on the expertise of the Web writer.
URL search	URL:thomas	Results will include all sites that contain thomas in the URL, if they have been selected by that search engine. Keep in mind, not all sites are collected on all search engines. Worth a try.
Domain search	Host:edu Domain:edu Site:edu	Combined with search words, you can limit a search to an educational site (or .gov, .mil, .org, etc.) Host, domain, and site are the three words to try. Different terms, same results.
Limit or enlarge a search	+aids +HIV -audiovisual -media -teacher	+ includes a word in the search, – excludes a search word. Do not use a space between the + or – and the search term. The example means, "I want AIDS & HIV, not other kinds of aids"
Search a phrase	"capital punishment"	Quotes keep your words together as a phrase. Some search engines have phrase detection, others not. To guarantee a phrase, use quotes.
Stack keywords, beginning with the most relevant	"student retention" "community colleges" statistics strategies	The most important terms here are student retention, then community colleges, etc. Many search engines will look for all terms, then begin to drop off terms from the right.
Wildcards or stemming	Sing*	Many search engines support truncation or wildcards. Sing* will search for words beginning with sing, including singing, sings, singer, single. Stemming actually includes endings and variations of words, e.g., swim* would find swimming and swam.
Expand your existing search		From an existing search, use value added commands like Related Searches, Related Sites, Find Similar, Within This Site, More From this Site.
Limit your existing search		From an existing search, use value added commands like Search within Results, Search these Results.

Peggy Whitley, peggy.whitley@nhmccd.edu
Sue Goodwin, sue.goodwin@nhmccd.edu
Catherine Olson, catherine.olson@nhmccd.edu
Phone: Work—281-312-1493; Fax—281-312-1450

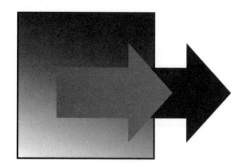

99 Jumpstarts
to Research

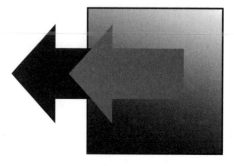

1 → ABORTION

Search Terms

Abortion

Pro-life

Pro-choice

Right to Life

Parental Rights and Abortion

Food for Thought

Abortion can be an emotional issue, with proponents from each side totally convinced that they are right, and with many unwilling to consider opposing viewpoints. Your argument will be more convincing if you avoid the emotional components and stick to the facts. Try to present both sides of the argument; then demonstrate why your position is preferable.

Because so much has been written, you should avoid information overload by narrowing your topic to one issue. Some possibilities are

⋏ Population control

⋏ Mother's health

⋏ Impaired fetus

⋏ RU 486

⋏ Rape or incest

⋏ Child mother

⋏ Parental rights of child under 18

⋏ Partial-birth abortion

⋏ Early termination of pregnancy

Background and Statistics

Abortion [Information Plus]

Abortion Decisions of the Supreme Court

Abortion, Medicine, and the Law

CQ Researcher (online version, *CQ Library,* also available)—*Abortion*

Current Issues & Enduring Questions

Great Cases in Constitutional Law

Issues & Controversies on File (online version, *Facts.com,* also available)

Opposing Viewpoints: Abortion

The Library Catalog

Abortion; Pro-life movement; Pro-choice movement

Magazines and Newspapers

Use a general database for public opinion.

ELECTRIC LIBRARY—*Abortion and* (*rape, China, ethics,* etc.)

PERIODICAL ABSTRACTS—*Abortion and* (*rape, China,* etc.)

For ethics and procedures, try a medical database. *Abortion, induced* is the most successful keyword:

CINAHL

MEDLINE—igm.nlm.nih.gov

HEALTH SOURCE PLUS

Internet

Pro-choice: National Abortion & Reproductive Rights Action—www.naral.org

National Organization of Women—www.now.org

Pro-life: National Right to Life Council—www.nrlc.org

U.S. Congress—thomas.loc.gov (for legislation)

Agencies to Contact

National Right to Life Action League, 419 7th St. NW, Suite 500,Washington, DC 20004

National Abortion & Reproductive Rights, 1156 15th St. NW, Suite 700, Washington, DC 20005

Related Jumpstarts

See Rape; Sex Education

2 ▶ AFFIRMATIVE ACTION

Search Terms

Affirmative Action

Quotas

Discrimination and (Job or Employ?)

Women (or Another Minority) and Employment

Equal Employment Opportunity Commission—EEOC

Food for Thought

Affirmative action began in the mid-twentieth century, when schools and employers were required to adopt policies that would make up for past discrimination. There is plenty of information; in fact, the biggest problem with this topic is that there is too much information. You can solve this problem by narrowing your topic to a specific minority group (gender, race), industry, or location. Also consider job discrimination against a religious group, people who are overweight, or the physically handicapped.

Examples: *affirmative action and African Americans* or *Hispanics and discrimination and (job or employ?)*.

Background and Statistics

CQ Researcher (online version, *CQ Library,* also available)

Interracial America: Opposing Viewpoints

Issues & Controversies on File (online version, *Facts.com,* also available)

The Legal Rights of Women

West's Encyclopedia of American Law

Women's Changing Role [Information Plus Series]

Your Rights in the Workplace

The Library Catalog

Affirmative Action; Employment—Discrimination

Magazines and Newspapers

Any general, newspaper, or business database will be helpful for this topic. Because there is so much on this topic, you might use the suggested keywords or combinations of them: *women (or another minority) and affirmative action.*

ABI INFORM. This business database is the best one to use.

PERIODICAL ABSTRACTS

INFOTRAC

ACADEMIC INDEX

ELECTRIC LIBRARY

Internet

U.S. Congress—thomas.loc.gov (for federal laws)

Equal Employment Opportunity Commission—www.eeoc.gov (for laws, complaint procedures, news)

United States Commission on Civil Rights—www.usccr.gov (an information clearinghouse dedicated to equal rights)

Megalaw—www.megalaw.com (to locate laws and cases by state; also includes federal law)

Cornell Law School—www.law.cornell.edu (for state statutes by broad topic or by state)

Also search *affirmative action* for sites in favor of that policy and *reverse discrimination* for sites opposed to it.

Agencies to Contact

Use the yellow pages for the local number of the Equal Employment Opportunity Commission (EEOC). Headquarters are at 1801 L St. NW, Washington, DC 20507, 1-800-669-4000

Related Jumpstarts

See Glass Ceiling; Political Correctness

3 → ALCOHOL ADVERTISING

Search Terms

Advertising and Alcohol and Legislature

Alcohol and Advertising

Drinking of Alcoholic Beverages

Voluntary Alcohol Advertising Standards for Children Act

Liquor

Food for Thought

Beer advertisements are synonymous with sports events. Some people watch the Super Bowl to see what Budweiser™ is doing next. What is the impact of advertising on alcohol consumption? Major issues include the following:

- Is advertising a major influence on underage drinking?
- Should advertisements be restricted to journals and television shows that children won't see?
- Has advertising created a subtle link between alcohol and sports?
- Is it fair or advantageous to require that equal time be given to anti-alcohol advertising?
- Should beer be treated the same as hard liquor? Should wine?

Answering any of these questions might give you enough information for a paper.

Background and Statistics

Alcohol: Opposing Viewpoints

Alcohol in Western Society from Antiquity to 1800

CQ Researcher

Encyclopedia of Drugs—Alcohol and Addictive Behavior

Substance Abuse Sourcebook

The Library Catalog

Alcoholism; Drinking of alcoholic beverages; Alcoholic beverage industry

Magazines and Newspapers

Any general, business, or medical index will be helpful, including

ELECTRIC LIBRARY

PERIODICAL ABSTRACTS—*Television advertising and liquor industry; advertising and liquor*

ABI INFORM—*Advertising and (alcohol or liquor)*

MEDLINE—igm.nlm.nih.gov

Internet

Try a keyword search for *alcohol advertising.* Possible sites include

Center for Science in the Public Interest—www.cspinet.org/booze/index.html—*BoozeNews Alcohol Policies Project*

Mothers Against Drunk Driving—www.madd.org (for statistics and discussion)

ChoiceMaster—www.choicemaster.com. Discusses a new type of alcohol advertising, through kiosks in malls.

Agencies to Contact

Center for Science in the Public Interest, 1875 Connecticut Ave. NW #300, Washington, DC 20009-5728, 202-332-9110, cspi@spinet.org

Center for Media Education, 1511 NW K St., Suite 518, Washington DC 20005, 202-628-2620, sp@cme.org

National Clearinghouse for Alcohol & Drug Information, PO Box 2345, Rockville, MD 20852, 1-800-729-6686, webmaster@health.org

Related Jumpstarts

See Drunk Driving; Media Influence on Public Opinion; Tobacco Regulations

4 ALTERNATIVE FUELS

Search Terms

Alternative Fuel

Alternative Energy Sources

Renewable Energy

Specific Fuel Sources

Food for Thought

Vehicles are a major consumer of oil, a fossil fuel. At the current rate of consumption, the world's oil resources will be gone in 100 years. You might argue whether we should be using or requiring alternative fuels, or you might consider which ones to try. What are the advantages and disadvantages of each type of fuel?

⌐ Is it renewable?

⌐ What is its effect on the environment?

⌐ Will it be affordable?

Some alternative fuels you might consider are hydrogen, methanol, natural gas, and solar power. Although electricity is not an alternative fuel in itself, electric or hybrid cars are an alternative use of current fuel.

Background and Statistics

Almanac of Renewable Energy

Alternative Fuels & the Environment

CQ Researcher (online version, *CQ Library,* also available)—*Alternative Fuels*

Issues & Controversies on File (online version, *Facts.com,* also available)—*Energy*

Renewable Energy

The Library Catalog

Power Resources; Renewable Energy Sources, Alternative Fuels, Electric Cars; Fossil Fuels; Energy Development

Magazines and Newspapers

Any general, business, or newspaper index will be helpful, such as

ELECTRIC LIBRARY

Newspapers online at www.usanewspapers.com or www.ecola.com/news/press

PERIODICAL ABSTRACTS

ABI INFORM

SIRS GOVERNMENT REPORTER

Internet

Department of Energy—www.eren.doe.gov. This is a particularly good site for energy efficiency and renewable energy.

American Petroleum Institute—www.api.org. (for energy facts and educational resources)

Agencies to Contact

National Alternative Fuels Hotline, 1-800-423-1363, hotline@afdc.nrel.gov

Related Jumpstarts

See Energy Sources; Green Companies

5 → ALTERNATIVE MEDICINE

Search Terms

Alternative Medicine

Herbal Remedies

Holistic

(Specific Treatments)

Food for Thought

Although most U.S. physicians limit their recommendations to traditional Western practices, other treatments have been used around the world for centuries. Folk medicine, Far Eastern medicine, and chiropractics all have their proponents.

⌐ Consider first: What is alternative medicine?

⌐ In what ways are particular treatments effective or ineffective?

⌐ Should these treatments be regulated?

⌐ Should health insurance cover alternative medicine?

⌐ Should physicians learn and include alternative treatments along with traditional medicine? If they do, should they inform patients?

To narrow your topic, you might choose one specific treatment, such as acupuncture, hypnosis, marijuana use, Reiki, meditation, homeopathic medicine, or holistic medicine. For others, check the *Alternative Health & Medicine Encyclopedia*, listed below.

Background and Statistics

Alternative Healing: The Complete A–Z Guide

Alternative Health & Medicine Encyclopedia

American Cancer Society's Guide to Complementary and Alternative Cancer Methods

CQ Researcher (online version, *CQ Library,* also available)—*Alternative Medicine*

PDR Family Guide to Natural Medicines and Healing Therapies

The Library Catalog

Alternative Medicine; Chiropractics; Holistic Medicine: Homeopathy; Naturopathy; Medicine, Oriental; Mental Healing

Magazines and Newspapers

Try a general or medical index, including the following:

ELECTRIC LIBRARY

PERIODICAL ABSTRACTS

CINAHL

MEDLINE—igm.nlm.nih.gov

HEALTH SOURCE PLUS

Internet

Alternative Medicine Homepage—www.pitt.edu/~cbw/altm.html (for conditions and treatments)

Food and Drug Administration—www.fda.gov. This site lists only those treatments for which the FDA has oversight.

National Institutes of Health—altmed.od.nih.gov/nccam. The National Center for Complementary and Alternative Medicine disseminates reliable information for consumers and practitioners.

Agencies to Contact

Alliance for Alternatives in Healthcare, PO Box 6279, Thousand Oaks, CA 91359-6279, Steve Gorman, President, 804-494-7818

National Center for Complementary and Alternative Medicine, National Institutes of Health, PO Box 8218, Silver Spring, MD 20907-8218, 1-888-644-6226

Related Jumpstarts

See FDA and Medicine Approval; Medicinal Uses of Marijuana

ANIMAL RESEARCH

Search Terms

Animal Research

Animal Testing, Animal Rights, Animal Welfare

PETA or Another Organization

AIDS (Tuberculosis) and Animal Research

Cosmetics and Animal Testing

Food for Thought

Although the use of animals in research can strike an emotional chord, you can write a more persuasive paper if you consider the topic from a scientific point of view. Consider alternatives such as computer models, testing on cell cultures, and human volunteers. The biomedical community attempts to use lesser species, such as rats rather than dogs; sea slugs rather than rats; or horseshoe crabs rather than rabbits.

- Should animals be used in developing new techniques and drugs? Why or why not? Are the results transferable to humans?

- Would you be willing to be the subject of a new treatment that has been developed on a computer and never tested on animals?

- Is it necessary to use animals in "cosmetic" and other product research?

Background and Statistics

Animal Experimentation

Animal Rights: Opposing Viewpoints

Animal Rights [Contemporary World Issues]

CQ Researcher (online version, *CQ Library,* also available)—*Medical Research* and *Animal Rights*

Issues & Controversies on File (online version, *Facts.com,* also available)—*Animals and Animal Rights*

The Library Catalog

Animal Welfare; Animal Rights; Animal Research

Magazines and Newspapers

Medical, science, and health indexes are best for this topic.

MEDLINE—igm.nlm.nih.gov

HEALTH SOURCE PLUS

For the human and local view, try general indexes and newspapers:

PERIODICAL ABSTRACTS—*Jeff Getty* (baboon bone marrow recipient and AIDS activist)

Newspapers online at www.usanewspapers.com or www.ecola.com/news/press

Your local newspaper

Internet

Watch out for bias on this hot topic. **NOTE**: Use *animal research* as your search term for a *positive* approach to animal research and *animal rights* for a negative approach.

American Anti-Vivisection Society—www.aavsonline.org

Anti-research: People for the Ethical Treatment of Animals (PETA)—www.peta-online.org

National Association for Biomedical Research—www.nabr.org

Pro-research: Americans for Medical Progress—www.amprogress.org

Agencies to Contact

PETA—People for the Ethical Treatment of Animals, 501 Front St., Norfolk VA 23510, 727-622-7382

Animal Welfare Information Center, 10301 Baltimore Ave., Beltsville MD 10705-2351, 301-504-6212, awic@nal.usda.gov

Related Jumpstarts

See Alternative Medicine; FDA and Medicine Approval

7 ➔ ASSISTED SUICIDE

Search Terms

Assisted Suicide and (Law or Legislation)
Assisted Suicide and Ethics
Death with Dignity Act
Euthanasia

Jack Kevorkian
Living Will
Right to Die
Terminally Ill

Food for Thought

Dr. Jack Kevorkian has been in the news for years for providing the terminally ill with the means to commit suicide. Is he a murderer or a hero? What ethical issues are at stake here? What legal ones? The courts are trying to decide if assisted suicide is really suicide or murder. Consider some of the following issues:

- ⌃ Do people have a right to die or an obligation to live?

- ⌃ Should the government interfere in this matter?

- ⌃ What are the alternatives to assisted suicide?

- ⌃ If assisted suicide becomes legal, what safeguards should be taken to ensure that only the terminally ill and not the temporarily depressed are aided in hurrying their demise?

Background and Statistics

CQ Researcher (online version, *CQ Library*, also available)

Death and Dying: Who Decides? [Information Plus Series]

Encyclopedia of Aging

Ethical and Legal Aspects of Nursing

Euthanasia [Contemporary World Issues]

Euthanasia: Opposing Viewpoints

Issues and Controversies on File (online version, *Facts.com*, also available)

Nurse's Legal Handbook

Physician Assisted Suicide

Physician's Assisted Suicide and Euthanasia

Terminal Illness: Opposing Viewpoints

The Library Catalog

Assisted Suicide; Euthanasia; Right to Die; Kevorkian

Magazines and Newspapers

Any general, newspaper, medical, or legal database will be useful, including

PERIODICAL ABSTRACTS

ELECTRIC LIBRARY

WASHINGTON POST or your local newspaper; especially good for Kevorkian

CINAHL

MEDLINE—igm.nlm.nih.gov

WESTLAW (for transcripts from Kevorkian trials)

Internet

Pro-euthanasia: The Hemlock Society—www.hemlock.org (for information about the right-to-die movement and maximizing options for a peaceful death)

Anti-euthanasia: International Anti-Euthanasia Task Force—www.iaetf.org (for world news on euthanasia practices and pain management)

Euthanasia.com—www.euthanasia.com (for statistics, articles and news)

Legislation:

Megalaw—www.megalaw.com (to locate laws and cases by state; also includes federal law)

Cornell Law School—www.law.cornell.edu (for state statutes by broad topic or by state)

Try a Metacrawler (www.metacrawler.com) search using *assisted suicide* or *terminally ill.*

Agencies to Contact

Hemlock Society, USA, PO Box 101810, Denver, CO 80250, 800-247-7421, hemlock@privatei.com

International Anti-Euthanasia Task Force, PO Box 760, Steubenville, OH 43952, 740-282-3810, info@iaetf.org

Related Jumpstarts

See Alternative Medicine; Medicinal Uses of Marijuana; Suicide in Elderly

ATHLETES AS ROLE MODELS

Search Terms

Conduct and Athletes

Conduct of Life and Athletes

Role Models and Athletes

(Sports or Athletes) and Salaries

Food for Thought

When a well-known athlete resorts to violence, it becomes a headline issue. Are athletes more prone to using drugs or violence than the general population? Do body-building drugs such as steroids cause shorter tempers? When an athlete accepts a multi-million-dollar contract, does it obligate him or her to be a role model for admirers?

You might consider the entire question of celebrities and the right to privacy, or narrow your topic to certain famous cases such as O. J. Simpson, Charles Barkley, Warren Moon, or Mike Tyson.

Background and Statistics

American Sport Culture

CQ Researcher (online version, *CQ Library*, also available)—*Sports*

Sports in America

Sports Ethics: A Reference Handbook

Sports in Society: Issues and Controversies

Sports Stars

The Library Catalog

Sports—Moral and ethical aspects

Magazines and Newspapers

This will be your best source of information. Try searching for *athletes and role models* or for information on specific athletes. Use any general index or newspaper index, such as

ACADEMIC INDEX

ELECTRIC LIBRARY

Newspapers online at www.usanewspapers.com or www.ecola.com/news/press

PERIODICAL ABSTRACTS

Internet

This is not the best source of information on this topic. If you use it, try the following:

Arthur Agee Role Model Foundation—www.edgesportsintl.com/arthur.htm. This foundation is dedicated to teaching adults how to be positive role models.

Role Model Project for Girls—www.womenswork.org/girls (for female role models from all fields)

Starseeker Sports Heroes—starseeker.com/sport.htm. If you're trying to find sports stars to research, this is a good starting point.

Related Jumpstarts

See Ethics of Political Leaders; Fitness for Children; Women's Athletics

ATTENTION DEFICIT HYPERACTIVITY DISORDER

Search Terms

Attention Deficit Disorder (ADD)

Attention Deficit Hyperactivity Disorder (ADHD)

Learning Disorders/Special Education

Ritalin and Effects

Adult Attention Deficit (or Adult ADD)

Food for Thought

Find a focus for this large topic. Parents are concerned that teachers who cannot deal with unruly students label them as ADD. Schools are concerned that the medication is not being given properly. This condition is so well known that the acronym alone will bring up plenty of information. It is better to use the complete term, however.

⋏ How does attention deficit hyperactivity disorder affect learning?

⋏ Are too many students taking Ritalin? Is it a cop-out for teachers? Parents? Doctors? What are the side effects with continual use?

⋏ Should people with ADHD be classified as disabled? Receive special education in school? Have special privileges? Take standardized tests?

⋏ What are the issues involved in adult ADD?

Background and Statistics

Diagnostic and Statistical Manual of Mental Disorders—DSM-IV

Diagnostic and Statistical Manual of Mental Disorders, Fourth Edition, Text Revision—DSM-IV-TR

Encyclopedia of Special Education

Macmillan Health Encyclopedia—Hyperactivity

The Library Catalog

Attention Deficit Disorder; Learning Disabilities; Hyperactivity; Adult Attention Deficit Disorder

Magazines and Newspapers

Try education and medical indexes, such as

MEDLINE—igm.nlm.nih.gov (for treatment or therapy, diagnosis, and medication)

ERIC—ericir.syr.edu/Eric (for ADHD students in the classroom and the resultant problems, assessment, and learning difficulties. Try ERIC Digest for a full text overview.)

PERIODICAL ABSTRACTS (indexes general articles on Ritalin and its effects)

Internet

National Institutes of Mental Health—www.nimh.nih.gov. Search within the site for government studies on ADHD.

University of Virginia—www.med.virginia.edu/medicine/clinical/pediatrics/devbeh/adhdlin/home.html. Basic scientific knowledge is presented, including classroom management, pharmacological treatment, and survival for parents.

National Attention Deficit Disorder Association—www.add.org/welcome1.html (for support groups, research, coaching, and personal stories)

Online newspapers—www.nhmccd.edu/contracts/lrc/kc/subjects.html#news

Agencies to Contact

Children and Adults with Attention Deficit Disorder (CHADD), 8181 Professional Place, Suite 201, Landover, MD 20785, 800-233-4050, www.chadd.org

National Attention Deficit Disorder Association (ADDA), PO Box 972, Mentor, OH 44061, 800-487-2282, mail@add.org

Related Jumpstarts

See Alternative Medicine; Fitness for Children

10 ➜ CAMPAIGN FINANCE REFORM

Search Terms

Campaign Contributions and Tax Deductible

Campaign Finance Reform

Soft Money

Food for Thought

Ex-President Bill Clinton was accused of inviting people to stay in the White House in exchange for contributions to the Democrat Party. Ralph Nader hoped to get 5 percent of the popular vote in the 2000 presidential election to qualify for federal campaign funds. Republican candidates for president dropped out of the race early because they could not compete with George W. Bush's fundraising. There are many issues to consider here.

- ⌐ Has fundraising become the focus of political parties, before ethics and issues?

- ⌐ What influence do major contributors have on political issues?

- ⌐ Should non-U.S. companies be allowed to donate to U.S. politicians? Or out-of state companies to local politicians?

- ⌐ Should giving be limited by dollar amounts?

- ⌐ Should people be allowed to fund themselves? Does this allow the rich more opportunity in politics?

Background and Statistics

Book of the States

Campaign Finance: The Reference Shelf

Congressional Quarterly

CQ Researcher (online version, *CQ Library,* also available)

Issues and Controversies on File (online version, *Facts.com,* also available)

Politics in America

The Library Catalog

Elections; Campaign Funds – United States

Magazines and Newspapers

Any general or newspaper index will be useful, such as

ACADEMIC INDEX

PERIODICAL ABSTRACTS—*Soft Money*

Your local newspaper; look for local politicians

WASHINGTON POST. This is the best of the databases because it reports action in Congress.

Internet

U.S. Congress—thomas.loc.gov. Check the *Congressional Record*. Search *Soft Money and Campaign Reform.*

Public Campaign—www.publicampaign.org. Identifies problems with the system and how to fix them.

Public Interest Research Groups—www.pirg.org. Choose *democracy/campaign finance reform* to get to Americans against Political Corruption.

Republican Party—www.rnc.org

Democrat Party—www.democrats.org

Agencies to Contact

Public Campaign, 1320 19th St. NW, Suite M-1, Washington, DC 20036, 202-293-0222, info@publicampaign.org

Related Jumpstarts

See Ethics of Political Leaders; Term Limits

11 → CAPITAL PUNISHMENT

Search Terms

Capital Punishment

Death Penalty

Visible Man

(Your state) and Death Penalty

Death Penalty and Women

Food for Thought

Capital punishment is an emotional issue, which you must try to evaluate objectively. Try to narrow the topic so you won't be overwhelmed with information and so that you present both sides of the issue. Possible subtopics are

- Is the death penalty cruel and unusual punishment?

- Does capital punishment deter murder?

- What is the purpose of the death sentence: prevention or punishment?

- Are a disproportionate number of blacks sentenced to death?

- Is it inhumane to hold a prisoner on death row for years?

- Should women be on death row?

- How likely is it that an innocent person could be executed? (See if you can find an example of this having occurred.)

Background and Statistics

Current Issues and Enduring Questions

Capital Punishment [Information Plus Series]

Complete History of the Death Penalty

Gallup Poll (monthly and annual issues available)

Capital Punishment: A Reference Handbook

The Rope, the Chair and the Needle

Real Life Dictionary of the Law

The Library Catalog

Capital Punishment

Magazines and Newspapers

All medical, news, and general indexes will be useful, including:

Newspapers. Look at local papers for local feeling about the issue.

ELECTRIC LIBRARY

PERIODICAL ABSTRACTS—*Capital Punishment and (morality, deterrent, ethics, etc.)*

HEALTH SOURCE PLUS. Contains articles on the role of physicians in capital punishment; administering the injection and pronouncing death.

Internet

Capital Punishment will bring good results, but most sites are anti-death penalty. Try:

ACLU Capital Punishment Project—www.aclu.org./ This is an anti-death penalty site, with news updates and death watch.

Justice for All—prodeathpenalty.com. This is a pro-death penalty site, with articles, news, and links.

American Society of Criminology—www.asc41.com. Go to the divisions for links to reliable sources of information.

Sourcebook of Criminal Justice Statistics—home.ubalt.edu/ntygsmit. Search for *death AND penalty.*

Megalaw—www.megalaw.com (to locate laws and cases by state; also includes federal law)

Cornell Law School—www.law.cornell.edu (for state statutes by broad topic or by state)

Agencies to Contact

National Coalition to Abolish the Death Penalty, 918 F St. NW, Suite 601, Washington, DC 20004, 888-286-2237, jzanon@ncapd.org

Justice Now, PO Box 1135, Columbus, GA 31902-1135

Related Jumpstarts

See Ethnic Cleansing; Human Rights of Prisoners

12 → CASHLESS SOCIETY

Search Terms

Debit Cards, Credit Cards, E-money

Cash Cards, Smart Cards, ATM

Electronic Commerce, Digital Cash

Electronic Funds Transfer

Electronic Benefit Transfer

Cashless Society

Food for Thought

Money has evolved. In the past, we had bartering, coins of valuable metals, paper representing those metals, and most recently paper based only on trust. Are we now headed for a moneyless society, in which financial wealth will be imbedded in a microchip? Has the electronic age influenced this development? The Internet has the most current and extensive coverage of this topic, although there is background information in books and journals.

Background and Statistics

Encyclopedia of Banking & Finance

CQ Researcher (online version, *CQ Library,* also available)—*Credit Cards*

Credit Cards and the Law

Issues & Controversies on File (online version, *Facts.com,* also available)—*Credit, consumer*

The Library Catalog

Electronic Funds Transfers; Paper Money; Credit Cards

Many books are available on this topic. Use a Title Keyword search for all of the terms listed above.

Magazines and Newspapers

News and business databases are best. Try

ELECTRIC LIBRARY—*Electronic Funds Transfer*

Your Local Newspaper—*Debit cards; Credit cards; ATM; Electronic Commerce*

PERIODICAL ABSTRACTS or ACADEMIC INDEX—*Electronic Commerce; Electronic funds transfer; Money; Smart Card*

ABI INFORM—*Electronic Commerce; Electronic Banking; Currency; Smart Cards.*

COMPUTER SELECT—*Electronic Funds Transfer* (keyword); *Electronic Cash Cards; Electronic Commerce*

Internet

Electric Money—www.nhmccd.edu/contracts/lrc/kc/e-money.html (for links to appropriate sites)

Bank for International Settlements—www.bis.org (for important articles and speeches by international bankers)

Green Book 2000—purl.access.gpo.gov/GPO/LPS4942. This is a guide for financial institutions.

U.S. Treasury—www.ustreas.gov. Search for *electronic money* for studies and trends.

U.S. Congress—thomas.loc.gov (for laws). Since Congress in 1996 mandated that government benefits would be paid only by electronic transfer starting in 1999, banks have been forced to create systems to accommodate this change.

Agencies to Contact

Consumer Action, 116 New Montgomery St., Suite 233, San Francisco CA 94105, 415-777-9648

Related Jumpstarts

See Mergers and Megacompanies

13 → CHANGING JOB MARKET

Search Terms

Blue Collar and White Collar and Workers and Change (a good search)

Careers

(Job or Employment) and (Security or Tenure or Scheduling)

Technology and Jobs and Change

Work Force and (Effects or Influences) and Change

Food for Thought

Downsizing and changes caused by technology and tenure are reshaping the face of the U.S. workforce. A thriving profession may become saturated with trained workers, forcing some to find a new field. The lines between blue-collar and white-collar workers are graying. In a short paper, select a single issue to write on or argue. Newspapers and journals will be the best source, although many books have good background information and statistics.

Background and Statistics

America Beyond 2001: Opposing Viewpoints

CQ Researcher (online version, *CQ Library*, also available)—*Wages & Salary; Employment*

Encyclopedia of Career Changes and Work Issues

Gallup Poll (monthly and annual issues available)

Into the Third Century [Information Plus Series]

Issues & Controversies on File (online version, *Facts.com*, also available)— Incomes and Income Gap; Labor & Employment

Occupational Outlook Handbook (also available online at stats.bls.gov/ocohome.htm)

Profile of the Nation [Information Plus Series]

The Library Catalog

Technology—Vocational Guidance; Workforce; Employees, Dismissal of; Organizational Change

Magazines and Newspapers

Use a business index first for best results. Also try any general or newspaper index, including:

ABI INFORM

Newspapers online at www.usanewspapers.com or www.ecola.com/news/press

PERIODICAL ABSTRACTS—*Jobs and Market and Change?; Blue Collar and White Collar and Work?*

Internet

This is a difficult topic to search on the Internet because the keywords aren't exact. Try the search words *changing job market.* Many of your results will include companies wanting to help you adapt.

Bureau of Labor Statistics—www.bls.gov/blshome.htm (for statistics). The section called "What's New" will give you the latest trends.

Occupational Outlook Handbook—www.bls.gov/ocohome.htm (for training, earnings, and job prospects for a wide range of fields)

Related Jumpstarts

See Dual Career Families; Mergers and Megacompanies

14 ➔ CHILD CARE

Search Terms

Employer Supported Day Care

Family and Medical Leave Act 1993

Child Care Services

Child Care and Employer

Food for Thought

Some studies suggest that good, quality child care can be more beneficial to children than staying at home with their mothers.

- ⅄ What constitutes good, quality child care?

- ⅄ Do employers have a stake in child care?

- ⅄ How much work time and productivity are lost when there is a lack of child care?

- ⅄ Might corporate downsizing affect employer-supported day care?

- ⅄ What are some alternative courses businesses can take to make child care easier for working parents?

Use statistics such as the percentage of single parents and dual-worker families, the changes in juvenile delinquency, standardized test scores, and absenteeism.

Background and Statistics

Statistical Record of Children

Women's Changing Roles [Information Plus Series]

Growing Up in America [Information Plus Series]

CQ Researcher (online version, *CQ Library*, also available)

Issues & Controversies on File (online version, *Facts.com*, also available)

The Library Catalog

Employer Supported Day Care; Children of Working Mothers

Magazines and Newspapers

Any newspaper or general database will have some information:

WASHINGTON POST. This provides full-text articles on day care centers, mostly dealing with abuse cases.

ELECTRIC LIBRARY. Look under Guided Search for *Day Care.*

PERIODICAL ABSTRACTS. Numerous articles from both popular and scholarly journals are included here. Sample search: *Day care and (child welfare or child care).*

Internet

National Organization of Women—www.now.org. Women's issues include child care. It may be a hot issue that appears when you open the page, or you may have to search within the site.

National Network for Child Care—www.nncc.org (for resources, newsletters, and an opportunity to ask questions)

ABC's of Safe and Healthy Child Care—www.cdc.gov/ncidod/hip/abc/abc.htm. This site is provided by the Centers for Disease Control.

National Child Care Information Center—nccic.org. This government-sponsored site includes statistics and publications.

Agencies to Contact

Child Care Action Campaign, 330 7th Ave., 17th Floor, New York, NY 10001 212-239-0138

National Resource Center for Health and Safety in Child Care, National Center for Education in Maternal and Child Health, Georgetown University, 2000 N. 15th St., Suite 701, Arlington, VA 22201-2617

Related Jumpstarts

See Dual Career Families; Flexible Work Schedules; Non-traditional Family

15 → CHILD LABOR

Search Terms

Child Labor

Sweatshops

Children Employment

(Mexico or another country) and Child Labor

Food for Thought

Children in some Third World countries are spending long hours making soccer balls and action figures for children in the United States to play with. They may sit at a sewing machine or stand at a loom all day for pennies, making designer clothing or carpets.

- ↳ What is our responsibility to these children?

- ↳ Are we helping them or harming them by buying the products they make?

- ↳ Should the United States refuse to do business with countries using child labor?

- ↳ Should individuals learn which companies employ child labor and boycott them?

- ↳ Are children being required to work here in the United States to help migrant farm families or those who do piece work at home?

Background and Statistics

By the Sweat and Toil of Children

Child Labor Is Not Cheap

CQ Researcher (online version, *CQ Library*, also available)—*Children*

Human Rights: Opposing Viewpoints

Issues & Controversies on File (online version, *Facts.com*, also available)—*Children*

The Library Catalog

Children employment

Magazines and Newspapers

Best results for this topic will be in a general index or newspaper, but you may also find information in an educational database.

ELECTRIC LIBRARY

Newspapers online at www.usanewspapers.com or www.ecola.com/news/press

PERIODICAL ABSTRACTS

ERIC—ericir.syr.edu/Eric. This is an educational database. Search term: *child labor.*

Internet

Bureau of International Labor Affairs—www.dol.gov/dol/ilab—International Child Labor Program

National Consumer's League—www.natlconsumersleague.org/—Child Labor Coalition

Stopping Child Labor through Education—members.nbci.com/childlabor/clmain .html. Includes history of child labor in the United States.

Agencies to Contact

Child Labor Coalition, National Consumers' League, 1701 K St. NW, Suite 1200, Washington, DC 10006, 202-835-3323, nclncl@aol.com

Child Labor Group, ILAB Room S-5303, US Dept. of Labor, Washington, DC 20210, 202-208-4843

Related Jumpstarts

See Human Rights of Prisoners; World Population and Hunger

16 ➡️ CLONING AND GENETIC RESEARCH

Search Terms

Bioethics

Biotechnology

Cloning

Clones

Genetic Engineering

Medical Ethics

Recombinant DNA

Stem Cell

Food for Thought

Genetic research is a multifaceted, controversial topic of growing concern. Although it applies to plants, human beings, and other animals, it becomes particularly controversial when applied to humans.

- ⅄ What are the ethical, moral, legal, and social issues to consider?

- ⅄ Do we make genetic modifications using modern biotechnology just because we can, or are we "playing God?"

- ⅄ Where should we draw the line: genetic engineering testing and cloning to cure or prevent diseases?

- ⅄ Will this result in more abortions or more suicides when someone is told they carry the gene for a terrible disease?

- ⅄ Will there be unfair discrimination based on differences such as sex, race, or income?

The landmark article about Dolly, the first successfully cloned mammal, is in *Nature,* February 27, 1997.

Background and Statistics

CQ Researcher (online version, *CQ Library,* also available)

Biomedical Ethics: Opposing Viewpoints

Encyclopedia of Bioethics

Genes

Genetic Engineering: Opposing Viewpoints

Issues and Controversies on File (online version, *Facts.com,* also available)— *Genes and Genetic Engineering*

Magill's Survey of Science

Statistical Record of Health and Medicine

The Library Catalog

Cloning; Molecular Cloning; Genetic Engineering; Recombinant DNA

Magazines and Newspapers

Use any general, medical, or newspaper index, including

PERIODICAL ABSTRACTS—*Clones and DNA; Genes, Genetics; Genetic Engineering and Ethics*

Newspapers online at www.usanewspapers.com or www.ecola.com/news/press

HEALTH SOURCE PLUS—*su(cloning)*

MEDLINE—igm.nih.nlm.gov. Search *Recombinant DNA;* the results are quite technical.

Internet

Try these sites or use a search engine with the search terms listed above.

New Scientist—www.newscientist.com/nsplus/insight/clone/clone.html (for news, facts, and forum)

Pharmaceutical Research & Manufacturers Association—www.phrma.org/genomics /cloning/index.html (for legislation, ethics, and research)

National Human Genome Research Institute—www.nhgri.nih.gov (for glossary, news, ethics, and grant information)

Related Jumpstarts

See Animal Research; Ethics and Organ Allocation

17 → COMMUNITY COLLEGE STANDARDS

Search Terms

Community Colleges

Junior Colleges

Two-year Colleges

Texas SB148 (transferability)

Food for Thought

Are community college standards as high as those of four-year colleges? Find statistics on the drop-out or success rates of community college students who transfer to a four-year college. Do all credits transfer? Should they? The criteria will vary by state.

What should be the purpose of a community college? What do you see as the future of the community college in the next century? You might want to include the reasons for choosing a community college rather than a four-year college:

- Cost
- Family obligations
- Availability of courses
- Bridge for high school underachievers
- Certificate courses

Background and Statistics

Academic Crisis of the Community College

Almanac of Higher Education

The Company We Keep

Digest of Educational Statistics

Encyclopedia of Educational Research

The Library Catalog

Community Colleges—United States; Industry and Education; Academic Achievement

Magazines and Newspapers

General, education, and business indexes will have some information.

Your local newspaper for local issues

PERIODICAL ABSTRACTS

ABI INFORM (for industry information)

ERIC—ericir.syr.edu/Eric—*Two-year colleges* and (*outcome of education* or *accountability*)

Internet

American Association of Community Colleges—www.aacc.nche.edu (for news and legislation)

League of Innovation in the Community College—www.league.org (for publications and conferences)

Department of Education—www.gseis.ucla.edu/ERIC/erictext.html—Clearinghouse for Community Colleges. Includes news, reports, and conferences.

Agencies to Contact

American Association of Community Colleges, National Center for Higher Education, 1 Dupont Circle NW, Suite 410, Washington, DC 20036-1176, 202-728-0200, mrivera@aacc.nche.edu

League of Innovation in the Community College, 26522 La Alameda, Suite 370, Mission Viejo, CA 92691, 714-367-2884

Related Jumpstarts

See Changing Job Market; Does a College Education Pay?

18 ➤ CRIME IN THE NEIGHBORHOODS

Search Terms

(Neighborhood or Suburb?) and Crime

Victim and (Neighborhood or Suburb)

Mall and Crime and (Plan or Program)

Food for Thought

This is a great narrowed topic (from crime). There are many resources, and you can find out what is going on close to home. The main body of materials will come from journals and newspapers, mostly because you want to get the newest information. Let's forget about gangs and deal with other crime.

This would be an opportunity to telephone your local mall manager and ask how mall security copes with crime, especially at busy shopping times of the year. He or she may be able to give you statistics. Watch the holiday papers for the list of hints shoppers can follow to keep from becoming victims.

⊿ What kinds of crimes are businesses experiencing?

⊿ What is management doing to make life safer for their businesses and for the customers who shop there? How can we keep from being victims as we walk to our cars?

Interview someone at your local police department about residential crime.

⊿ Ask about trends and prevention and arrest rates.

⊿ Ask what kinds of crimes neighborhoods are contending with.

⊿ Ask how they are dealing with these crimes.

Background and Statistics

CQ Researcher (online version, *CQ Library*, also available)—*Suburban Crime*

Crime [Information Plus Series]

Uniform Crime Reports for the United States—www.fbi.gov/ucr.htm

County & City Data Book (for statistics)

The Library Catalog

Crime prevention—United States. This will require looking for circulating books. There are plenty on crime in general. Use the book's index to determine if the book is right for your topic.

Look up *suburb?* as a heading and find books about suburbs and neighborhoods.

Magazines and Newspapers

Try business, general, and newspaper indexes, including:

ABI INFORM. Use this database if you decide to research what businesses are doing to contend with neighborhood crime.

PERIODICAL ABSTRACTS. Look here for magazines with articles about neighborhood watch, suburban crime, and anything about neighborhoods.

Your local newspaper. Great for the business and local view of neighborhood crime.

Internet

Bureau of Juvenile Statistics—www.ojp.usdoj.gov/bjs (for statistics and key facts)

Uniform Crime Reports—www.fbi.gov/ucr.htm. Look particularly in programs and initiatives.

Neighborhood Crime Watch Programs will yield lots of information on programs in different communities.

Any shopping mall on the Web will have information. Search for your local mall or police department.

Related Jumpstarts

See Gangs; Youth Crime

19 ▶ CRIMES AGAINST THE ELDERLY

Search Terms

(Old or Elderly or Aged)

Elderly Victims

Abuse and Elderly and (Physical, Mental, Psychological, Material, etc.)

Violent Crime and Elderly (might use a specific crime, like Aggravated Assault)

Scams and Elderly

Elder Abuse

Food for Thought

The elderly are at a higher risk of victimization by both strangers and family. Strangers perpetrate scams, assault, robbery, and rape. Crime or abuse by persons known to the elderly can be psychological, physical, material, or financial. These crimes are committed generally by members of the family or by caregivers. Is failure to give adequate pain medication to the elderly considered to be abuse? Decide on the focus your argument or research will take; then select keywords. There is plenty of information on all aspects of this broad topic.

Background and Statistics

Growing Old in America [Information Plus Series]

Crime [Information Plus Series]—*Age.* A bit about scams is included here.

Domestic Violence [Information Plus Series]

The Encyclopedia of Aging

Uniform Crime Reports for the United States—www.fbi.gov/ucr.htm

The Library Catalog

Aged – Crimes Against; Abused Aged

Magazines and Newspapers

Any general or newspaper index will have plenty of information on this topic.

ELECTRIC LIBRARY

Your local newspaper. If you are looking for local information, this is a good source.

Newspapers online at www.usanewspapers.com or www.ecola.com/news/press

PERIODICAL ABSTRACTS. This huge database will probably be your best source.

Internet

Department of Justice—www.ojp.usdoj.gov/bjs (for statistics and reports). There is a report called *Crimes against the Elderly.*

American Bar Association—www.seniorlaw.com/resource.htm (for elder abuse, regulations, and resources)

Department of Health and Human Services Administration on Aging—www.aoa.dhhs .gov/default.htm (for elder abuse prevention, resources, and statistics)

Related Jumpstarts

See Crime in the Neighborhoods

20 → CRIMINAL PSYCHOLOGY

Search Terms

Crime and Causes

Criminal Psychology

Forensic Psychiatry

Forensic Psychology

Psychology, Pathological

Food for Thought

Consider the how, why, who, background, and causes for behavior of criminals. What makes one person become an upstanding citizen, while another in seemingly identical circumstances turns to crime? Forensic psychology is a relatively new field of study that examines questions like these. Most of your information will be found in journals.

Background and Statistics

CQ Researcher (online version, *CQ Library,* also available)—*Crime and Criminals*

Encyclopedia of Crime and Justice—Forensic Psychology

Encyclopedia of Criminology and Deviant Behavior

Encyclopedia of Psychology—Forensic Psychology

The Library Catalog

Criminal Psychology; Forensic Psychology; Psychology, Pathological

Magazines and Newspapers

Try general and medical indexes, including

ACADEMIC INDEX

PERIODICAL ABSTRACTS

CINAHL

HEALTH SOURCE PLUS

MEDLINE—igm.nlm.nih.gov—*Criminal Psychology; Antisocial Personality Disorder*

Internet

Search the words *Forensic Psychology* for best results, or try the following sites:

American Psychology Law Society—www.unl.edu/ap-ls

University of Calgary—www.forensiceducation.com/index1.htm. This covers forensic nursing education, with journals, glossary, timelines, and statistics.

Medicine, Psychiatry and Forensic Expert—www.forensic-psych.com. A forensic expert discusses the field.

American Psychological Association—www.apa.org. Search the site for abstracts of articles and books on criminal psychology.

Agencies to Contact

American College of Forensic Psychiatry, PO Box 5870, Balboa Island, CA 92662, 714-831-0236

American Academy of Forensic Psychology, 128 N. Craig St., Pittsburgh, PA 15213, 412-681-3000, aafp@abfp.com

Related Jumpstarts

See Human Rights of Prisoners; Police Brutality

21 ⟶ CULTS

Search Terms

Alternative Religious Cults

Aum Shivriko (Japanese cult)

Cults and Psychology

Heaven's Gate

Waco or Branch Davidians

Food for Thought

According to the *American Heritage Dictionary of the English Language* (3d ed.), a *cult* is a religious sect generally considered to be extremist or false. Its followers are under the guidance of an authoritarian, charismatic leader, and are often living communally.

Consider the following questions:

⋏ Are cults protected by Freedom of Religion?

⋏ What rights have others (parents, authorities) to try to bring cult members back into the mainstream?

⋏ What methods are used to reclaim these members? Are they legal? Does the end justify the means?

⋏ Are cults dangerous to society? To their members?

Background and Statistics

Biographical Dictionary of American Cult and Sect Leaders

CQ Researcher (online version, *CQ Library*, also available)

Encyclopedic Handbook of Cults in America

Encyclopedia of New Age Beliefs

Encyclopedia of Social Work

Extremist Groups: Opposing Viewpoints

Issues and Controversies on File (online version, *Facts.com*, also available)—*Cults*

New Age Encyclopedia

The Library Catalog

Cults; Psychology, Religious

Magazines and Newspapers

Use any general, newspaper, or medical index, including

ACADEMIC INDEX

ELECTRIC LIBRARY—*Cults* or names of specific groups

CINAHL (for mental health of cult members)

PERIODICAL ABSTRACTS

Internet

The World Wide Web will have much information on cults. Be careful where you get your information—be sure it is a valid source and that you have all the information you need for citing the work. Use the suggested search terms or try the following sites:

Ontario Consultants on Religious Tolerance—www.religioustolerance.org. This site presents cults as new or different religious groups.

AFF Cult Group information—www.csj.org. Covers recruitment, conversion, and exiting cult groups.

Agencies to Contact

American Family Foundation, PO Box 2265, Bonita Springs, FL 34133, 212-533-5420, aff@worldnet.att.net

Related Jumpstarts

See Gangs; Rape

22 → CULTURAL HERITAGE

Search Terms

Cultural Diversity

Cultural Heritage Allegiance

Culture and Prejudice

Ethnic Identity

Immigrants and Assimilate

Melting Pot

Multiculturalism

Immigration and Adjustment

Food for Thought

Not too long ago, immigrants became completely assimilated into our society and attempted to lose their own ethnic identity. Today, people from different ethnic backgrounds feel that it is important to preserve their history. Large ethnic groups living together are a force to be considered. As immigrant populations reach a critical mass, especially in large cities, is the "melting pot" transforming them, or are they transforming U.S. society? What will the impact of these groups be in the future? This is a great topic. Try to put yourself in both situations (as an immigrant and as a native born person) so you can see both sides of this issue. Consider the following:

- Should immigrants be forced to assimilate into U.S. society? If they do not, do they still realize the American dream?

- Is the huge influx of immigrants into U.S. cities causing "white flight?" If so, how will this affect present and the future assimilation of these immigrants into U.S. society?

- In what ways does the influx of poor immigrants strain municipal budgets? What should be done?

- In what ways should people of different nationalities integrate into the community? Should they retain their own cultural differences?

- How should adjustment to a new country be evaluated?

- Does an ethnic neighborhood of the twenty-first century invite prejudice?

- How is the diversity of many peoples a positive force in U.S. society? A negative force?

You might want to read the following excellent online series from *The Washington Post* as background: www.washingtonpost.com/wp-srv/national/longterm/meltingpot /melt0222.htm.

Background and Statistics

CQ Researcher (online version, *CQ Library*, also available)

Immigration and Illegal Aliens [Information Plus Series]

Interracial America: Opposing Viewpoints

Issues & Controversies on File (online version, *Facts.com*, also available)

Kiss, Bow and Shake Hands

Minorities: A Changing Role in American Society [Information Plus Series]

Culture Wars: Opposing Viewpoints

The Library Catalog

Ethnicity; Racial Prejudice; Minorities; Multiculturalism; Ethnic Identity

Magazines and Newspapers

Use a general database for public opinion. Newspapers are a good source for this topic. Consider ERIC, the education database. If you want to look at just one area of the country, find a local newspaper.

ELECTRIC LIBRARY

PERIODICAL ABSTRACTS

EBSCO HOST

NEWSPAPERS online—www.ecola.com

ERIC—ericir.syr.edu/Eric. Use *immigration and assimilation* as keywords.

Internet

The Internet can be a good source. Use the keywords above or some about your own or a selected ethnic group.

Ask Jeeves—www.askjeeves.com. Use natural language, for example, *"How should immigrants assimilate into American society?"* Jeeves is pretty good at answering questions like these.

Smithsonian Folklore and Cultural Heritage Center—www.folklife.si.edu

Cultural Profiles Project—cwr.utoronto.ca/cultural/english/index.html. This wonderful project is Canadian but offers profiles on people from many countries.

U.S. Census Bureau—www.census.gov. Get the facts and stats. This is a good place to look for information on poverty levels of ethnic groups.

Agencies to Contact

National Urban League, 120 Wall St., New York, NY 212-558-5300, www.nul.org

National Center for Neighborhood Enterprise, 1424 16th St. NW, Washington, DC 20036, www.ncne.com

Related Jumpstarts

See Affirmative Action; Illegal Immigration

23 → CURFEWS

Search Terms

Curfew

Juvenile Delinquents

Civil Rights and Curfew

Food for Thought

Curfews originated in England in the eleventh century. When the church bells rang at 8:00 P.M., all fires were to be extinguished and the people had to go to bed. This rule was established to prevent insurrection and had the added benefit of diminishing the chance of fire, which could destroy a whole village. Nowadays curfews are established to prevent juvenile delinquency. Is this a violation of teenagers' rights or a good solution to a growing problem? Is it discrimination? Consider the various laws.

Curfews for all ages are also used to deter crime in areas of civil unrest. They can be instituted after a natural disaster such as a hurricane or a fire. In war-torn countries they might be used to control conspiracy. Is a curfew defensible under these circumstances?

A comparison of curfews could help justify your position.

Background and Statistics

CQ Researcher (online version, *CQ Library,* also available)

Guide to American Law

Issues and Controversies on File (online version, Facts.com, also available)

Teen Legal Rights

Your own state laws, available at most public libraries

The Library Catalog

Curfew; Juvenile Delinquency. Very little is available.

Magazines and Newspapers

Try a general or newspaper index such as the following:

ELECTRIC LIBRARY

Newspapers online at www.usanewspapers.com or www.ecola.com/news/press

PERIODICAL ABSTRACTS

Internet

Student interest site—www.oblivion.net. This site fights age-based discrimination.

American Civil Liberties Union—www.aclu.org (for news and statistics). Use the "search" button.

U.S. Congress—thomas.loc.gov (for relevant laws)

Megalaw—www.megalaw.com (to locate laws and cases by state; also includes federal law)

Cornell Law School—www.law.cornell.edu (for state statutes by broad topic or by state)

Related Jumpstarts

See Drug Testing in the Workplace; Gangs

DIVORCE— NO-FAULT

24

Search Terms

Divorce

No-Fault Divorce

Divorce Rate

Irreconcilable Differences

Food for Thought

Under no-fault divorce, which exists in most states, fault on the part of either spouse need not be shown or proved. One or both parties simply claim either "irreconcilable" differences or that the marriage has "irretrievably" broken down.

- ⅄ Is this too easy?
- ⅄ How has no-fault divorce affected the family?
- ⅄ What role should religious institutions and the government play in divorce?
- ⅄ What is the history of no-fault divorce?
- ⅄ What are its advantages and disadvantages?
- ⅄ What is the law about divorce in your state? How does it compare to other states?

Background and Statistics

CQ Researcher (online version, *CQ Library*, also available)

Encyclopedia of Marriage and the Family.

The Family: Opposing Viewpoints

Marriage, Family, and Relationships: A Cross-Cultural Encyclopedia

The Library Catalog

Divorce, Laws and Regulations; No-fault Divorce

Magazines and Newspapers

Use any general or newspaper index, including

PERIODICAL ABSTRACTS—*Divorce and (children; no-fault; statistics)*

ELECTRIC LIBRARY (for journal articles and transcripts of television and radio shows)

Newspapers online at www.usanewspapers.com or www.ecola.com/news/press

Internet

Try Metacrawler at www.metacrawler.com and search for *No-fault divorce.*

National Organization of Women—www.now.org. Search for *no-fault divorce* for legislation and articles.

Divorce Source—www.divorcesource.com/info/divorcelaws/states.shtml (for state laws abbreviated)

Divorce information by state—www.divorce-bankrupt.com/divorce.html. This is a commercial site, but it has some good information.

Megalaw—www.megalaw.com (to locate laws and cases by state; also includes federal law)

Cornell Law School—www.law.cornell.edu (for state statutes by broad topic or by state)

Agencies to Contact

Marriage Savers, 9500 Michael's Court, Bethesda, MD 20817, 301-469-5870

Family Research Council, 700 13th St., Suite 500, Washington, DC 20005, 202-393-2100

American Association for Marriage and Family Therapy, 1133 15th St. N.W., Suite 300, Washington, DC 20005, 202-452-0109

Related Jumpstarts

See Child Care; Non-traditional Family

25 → DOES A COLLEGE EDUCATION PAY?

Search Terms

Earnings

Education and [other words in this section]

Pay

Salaries

Wages

Food for Thought

How important is a college education? It takes at least four years to earn a bachelor's degree, four years during which the student is spending money rather than earning it. Does one need a college education to be financially successful? Does it really make a difference in earnings, or would four years of experience be more advantageous? Is education imperative to get and keep a particular job? What are the long-term financial rewards? Find hard statistics for this topic.

Background and Statistics

CQ Researcher (online version, *CQ Library,* also available)—*College Graduates—employment*

Digest of Educational Statistics. Contains statistics on outcomes of education. Good charts.

Education [Information Plus Series]

Issues & Controversies on File (online version, *Facts.com,* also available)—*Education*

Occupational Outlook Handbook—stats.bls.gov/ocohome.htm. Covers job training requirements and salaries.

The Library Catalog

Education—Economic Aspects; Wages—United States

Magazines and Newspapers

Journal and newspaper articles are best for this topic. You will find many articles that are not on the topic, but it is impossible to weed them out using the suggested keywords, so choose carefully.

Use any general, newspaper, business, or educational index, including

PERIODICAL ABSTRACTS. Some articles have dollar amounts and rankings about education versus non-education in the workplace.

ABI INFORM. Try *(labor or job or employment) and education and (pay or salary)*. Some articles are about the advantages of businesses training or educating employees to do a better job, which results in a salary increase. This is a little off the subject, but interesting.

ERIC—ericir.syr.edu/Eric. Don't be tempted to get too fancy. A very successful search was (one word on each line) *salary, high school, education.*

Internet

Some results may be obtained with a search for *value of college education,* but this is not a good topic for the Internet. Using *college* as a search term is not as successful as *education* because you are researching the amount of education. You get into articles about costs of college when you use *college* or *university.* However, it never hurts to try many keyword combinations. You may find some information at

The National Center for Educational Statistics—nces.ed.gov/edstats (for both current statistics and projections to 2010)

Related Jumpstarts

See Changing Job Market; Community College Standards

26 DOWNTOWN: CAN IT BE SAVED?

Search Terms

(Your town) and History

Downtown Renovation

Urban Beautification

Urban Planning

Urban Renewal

Food for Thought

Suburban sprawl has taken many better-paid, better-educated families out of the city, leaving behind those who cannot afford to move. Many stores and businesses have followed, leaving city downtowns devastated. Is there any hope for the cities?

- What are the proposals for renovation in your town? Is spending tax dollars for such renovation a wise use of resources?

- Will this renovation bring money into the city? Revitalize downtown?

- How successful have downtown renewals been in other major cities? Compare your city with other urban renewal projects. (Denver and Baltimore are good examples.)

- Compare cities and suburbs.

- Consider the effect of malls and superstores like Wal-Mart™ on downtown businesses.

Background and Statistics

Cities of the United States. Development projects are listed under each city.

CQ Researcher (online version, *CQ Library,* also available)—*Cities and Towns*

Issues & Controversies on File (online version, *Facts.com,* also available)—*Cities, US*

Land and the City: Patterns and Processes of Urban Change

Magazines and Newspapers

Use a general or business database such as one of the following:

ABI INFORM. Provides general information about "white flight" or urban renewal.

Your local newspaper. A local newspaper will be the best place to find specifics.

PERIODICAL ABSTRACTS

Internet

This may be useful for specific cities. For keywords, try *Downtown Renovation* or *Urban Planning* and your town's name.

Department of Housing and Urban Development—www.hud.gov. Covers government programs, aimed mainly at affordable housing.

Council for Urban Economic Development—www.cued.org/research (for research and statistics)

Related Jumpstarts

See Sports Arenas; Superstores

27 ➤ DRESS CODES

Search Terms

Dress Codes

School Uniforms

School and Uniforms and Behavior

Food for Thought

Do clothes make the person? Some schools are turning to school uniforms to downplay differences among students. These differences could be cultural, economic, or social. At the same time, businesses that have had dress codes are now more casual. There are many ideas to consider in this topic.

- Do uniforms improve attitudes and behavior in the public schools?

- Do school uniforms infringe on students' rights to personal expression?

- Can school uniforms decrease violence in schools?

- What is the federal government's policy toward school uniforms?

- Do uniforms create a sense of unity in the workplace?

- How about pro-facto uniforms, such as everyone wearing a business suit to work?

- Does casual dress in the workplace promote a casual attitude toward the work being done?

Be sure to consider the psychological studies.

The Library Catalog

Dress Codes

Background and Statistics

CQ Researcher (online version, *CQ Library,* also available)

Issues and Controversies on File (online version, *Facts.com,* also available)

John T. Malloy's New Dress for Success

John T. Malloy's New Women's Dress for Success

Magazines and Newspapers

An educational index is best.

ERIC—ericir.syr.edu/Eric. Look here first for school uniforms, because this index devotes itself to education, and the studies and articles listed are written by experts on education.

Also try a business or general database:

ABI INFORM (for articles about business dress codes)

PERIODICAL ABSTRACTS—*School uniforms; Dress Codes*

Newspapers online at www.usanewspapers.com or www.ecola.com/news /press

Internet

U.S. Department of Education—www.ed.gov.sp. Includes a manual on school uniforms.

Try searching for *Dress codes* or *school uniforms* in a search engine such as metacrawler.com or www.about.com.

Agencies to Contact

Editorial Projects in Education, Inc., 4301 Connecticut Ave. NE, Suite 250, Washington, DC 20008, 202-364-4114, webster@epe.org

Related Jumpstarts

See Drug Testing in the Workplace; School Violence

28 → DRINKING ON CAMPUS

Search Terms

Alcoholism

Alcohol and (Campus or College Student)

Binge Drinking

Drinking and Higher Education

Student Drinking

Food for Thought

Drinking alcoholic beverages has become a rite of passage for young adults. College students seem especially to participate in binge drinking.

- ⋏ What drives students to drink?
- ⋏ Should alcohol be allowed on campus?
- ⋏ Is a college responsible for the behavior of its students?
- ⋏ What responsibilities do the drinking student's friends have?
- ⋏ Do fraternities and sororities contribute to the problem?
- ⋏ Would a "safe place" such as a bar on campus help control or encourage drinking problems?
- ⋏ Does binge drinking when young predispose one to alcoholism?

Background and Statistics

Alcohol and Tobacco [Information Plus Series]

CQ Researcher (online version, *CQ Library*, also available)—*Alcohol*

Issues & Controversies on File (online version, *Facts.com*, also available)—*Alcohol*

The Library Catalog

Alcohol Drinking in Adolescence; Drinking of Alcoholic Beverages; College Students—Alcohol Use; College Students—Conduct of Life

Magazines and Newspapers

PERIODICAL ABSTRACTS—*Alcohol Use and College*

ERIC—ericir.syr.edu/Eric

HEALTH SOURCE PLUS—*College Students—Alcohol Use; Drinking of Alcoholic Beverages—Universities and Colleges*

MEDLINE—igm.nlm.nih.gov

Internet

U.S. Department of Education—www.ed.gov (for reports and statistics)

National Clearinghouse for Alcohol & Drug Information—www.health.org—*Prevention Online*

Mothers Against Drunk Driving—www.madd.org. Choose *Under 21.*

Search *campus alcohol* for policies at individual schools.

Agencies to Contact

U.S. Department of Education, 400 Maryland Ave. SW, Washington, DC 20202–0498, 1-800-USA-LEARN

Related Jumpstarts

See Alcohol Advertising; Drunk Driving; Rape

29 → DRUG TESTING IN THE WORKPLACE

Search Terms

Drug Abuse and Employ?

Drug Testing and Workplace

Employees and Drug Testing

Workplace Privacy

Food for Thought

Many businesses require pre-employment drug testing, or they may make random checks of employees. Consider some of the implications:

- Is mandatory drug testing an invasion of a worker's privacy?

- Is drug testing an effective deterrent to illegal drug use?

- Should a worker be reprimanded or punished for something he or she does on private time?

- How accurate are drug tests?

- Should drug tests be given randomly or only when there is indication of abuse?

- Should those with certain critical jobs be subject to tougher scrutiny? Consider doctors, pilots, bus drivers, and air traffic controllers.

Background and Statistics

CQ Researcher (online version, *CQ Library*, also available)—*Drug Abuse—Testing*

Drug Abuse: Opposing Viewpoints

Drugs, Drug Testing and You

Drug Testing: Issues and Options

Drugs Workplace Testing

Encyclopedia of Drugs—Alcohol, and Addictive Behavior

The Gallup Poll

Issues & Controversies on File (online version, *Facts.com*, also available)—*Drugs and Drug Abuse*

War on Drugs: Opposing Viewpoints

The Library Catalog

Employees Drug Use; Employee Rights; Drugs and Employment; Drug Abuse Prevention

Magazines and Newspapers

Use any general, business, or newspaper index, including

ELECTRIC LIBRARY

Newspapers online at www.usanewspapers.com or www.ecola.com/news/press

WASHINGTON POST or any other newspaper

PERIODICAL ABSTRACTS

ABI-INFORM

Internet

American Civil Liberties Union—www.aclu.org. Provides anti-testing information.

National Clearinghouse for Alcohol & Drug Information—www.health.org—Prevention Online (pro-testing information).

Institute for a Drug Free Workplace—www.drugfreeworkplace.org

Agencies to Contact

American Civil Liberties Union (ACLU), 122 Maryland Ave., NE, Washington, DC 20002, 202-544-1681

Institute for a Drug Free Workplace, 202-842-7400, nndelogu@littler.com

Related Jumpstarts

See Curfews; Dress Codes

30 > DRUNK DRIVING

Search Terms

Alcohol and Accidents

Alcohol Intoxication

Drunk Driving

DWI

Food for Thought

For years, Mothers Against Drunk Driving (MADD) has been lobbying to enact tougher drunk driving standards, and their efforts are making inroads. States that don't comply with federal standards may have federal highway funds withheld.

⌐ What is the current legal definition of drunk driving in your state? Are the current laws too strict or too lenient? Why?

⌐ Should we allow people to drink and drive but punish them more severely when they have an accident?

⌐ Do open container laws help curtail drinking and driving?

⌐ Should drunk drivers, like drug dealers, have their vehicles confiscated?

⌐ What other options might there be to the current laws?

You might approach this as a state-to-state comparison or as a states' rights issue. You might also look at the laws in other countries.

Background and Statistics

CQ Researcher (online version, *CQ Library,* also available)—*Drunken Driving*

Drunk Driving Law

Injury Facts

Issues & Controversies on File (online version, *Facts.com,* also available)—*Alcohol and Alcohol Abuse*

National Survey of State Laws

The Library Catalog

Drunk Driving; Drinking and Traffic Accidents; Traffic Violations

Magazines and Newspapers

Medical and general databases will have some information:

ELECTRIC LIBRARY

PERIODICAL ABSTRACTS

CINAHL—*Driving and Alcohol Intoxication*

MEDLINE—igm.nlm.nih.gov—*Alcohol? and Accidents*

Internet

Mothers Against Drunk Driving—www.madd.org

Insurance Institute for Highway Safety—www.highwaysafety.org (for statistics)

Centers for Disease Control—www.cdc.gov/ (for statistics and programs)

Megalaw—www.megalaw.com (to locate laws and cases by state; also includes federal law)

Cornell Law School—www.law.cornell.edu (for state statutes by broad topic or by state)

Agencies to Contact

Mothers Against Drunk Driving, 18935 North IH45, Houston, TX 77388, 800-261-6233, info@madd.org

Related Jumpstarts

See Alcohol Advertising; Drinking on Campus

31 → DUAL CAREER FAMILIES

Search Terms

Dual Career

Dual Income

Work and Family

Working Mothers

Food for Thought

What impact have two-career families had on society? Some areas of impact are

- ⌐ Shopping: Some stores are now open 24 hours a day, more people are shopping online, and groceries can be delivered.

- ⌐ Eating out (find statistics).

- ⌐ Handling sick family members.

- ⌐ Getting repairs done.

- ⌐ Who is doing the housework and/or raising the children? Has this changed the attitudes of women toward men and vice versa?

- ⌐ What are the costs of employment?

- ⌐ Find statistics on the real value of the second income after subtracting the costs of employment.

- ⌐ What is the impact on children/families?

Job transfers are also an issue. When one spouse has an attractive offer but has to relocate, what should the other do?

Background and Statistics

Statistical Abstract of the United States

Official Guide to the American Marketplace—Impact on businesses

Official Guide to American Attitudes—Opinion polls

Encyclopedia of Marriage and the Family

Statistical Handbook on the American Family

The Library Catalog

Dual Career Families; Work and Family

Magazines and Newspapers

Use any general, newspaper, education, or business index, such as

ELECTRIC LIBRARY—*Working women*

PERIODICAL ABSTRACTS—*Dual Career Couples; Women & employment; Women & labor force*

WASHINGTON POST—*Working mothers*

ABI INFORM—*Working mothers; dual career couples*

ERIC—ericir.syr.edu/Eric—*Dual Career Family; Employed women*

Internet

Search the keywords *dual earner* or try the following sites:

The Alfred P. Sloan Foundation—www.sloan.org/main.htm. This organization is a major researcher on this subject.

Dual Career Network—www.uiowa.edu/~provost/dcn/index.html. This service helps academic couples find employment together.

Agencies to Contact

WomenWork!, 1625 K St. NW, Suite 300, Washington, DC 20006, 1-800-235-2732

Alfred P. Sloan Foundation, 6330 Fifth Ave., Suite 2550, New York, NY 10011-0242, christensen@sloan.org

Related Jumpstarts

See Changing Job Market; Child Care

32 ➡ DUAL ENROLLMENT

Search Terms

Concurrent Enrollment

Dual (Credit or Enrollment)

College Credit and High School

Cooperative Programs and College

. . . and Results

Food for Thought

Dual credit/dual enrollment/concurrent enrollment. These terms refer to college credit for high school students who take college classes instead of high school ones and get credit for both. This option is becoming more available. One of the most attractive benefits of taking early credit is that it saves money on college costs. A student can conceivably enter college with 15 or more credits. On the other hand, a student may find the college class too difficult and be unable to graduate from high school on schedule. Although there is not much information on this topic in the general databases, ERIC has more than enough for a great debate on this issue.

- ⅄ Do students learn everything they need if they take one class rather than two? (College history rather than high school history before college history.)

- ⅄ Are students emotionally and mentally ready to learn at a college level when they are still in high school?

- ⅄ Are the rules and standards the same for the student taking a college class through high school as they would be at the college?

- ⅄ What are some of the benefits or disadvantages of a program like this?

- ⅄ Is the student really receiving a college-level education? What does the research say about students who have completed college after participating in these dual programs?

- ⅄ Is this method appropriate for every discipline? Are there some subjects that should not be taught in this way? Why or why not?

The Library Catalog

College Credits

Magazines and Newspapers

Use any education database, including

ERIC—ericir.syr.edu/Eric. This is the best place to look for this information. Try *ERIC Digest* for an overview.

Internet

Keyword searching for *Dual Enrollment and High School* will link you to many excellent sites, particularly first-hand information on the districts and colleges that participate in this program and their reports.

Megalaw—www.megalaw.com (to locate laws and cases by state; also includes federal law)

Cornell Law School—www.law.cornell.edu (for state statutes by broad topic or by state)

Agencies to Contact

Contact a local school district that offers dual enrollment to its students.

Related Jumpstarts

See Community College Standards; Does a College Education Pay?

EATING DISORDERS: ANOREXIA AND BULIMIA

Search Terms

Eating Disorders

Anorexia or Anorexia Nervosa

Bulimia

Bulimarexia

Compulsive Eating

Food for Thought

Anorexia nervosa is characterized by fear of obesity and resulting in severe weight loss. Bulimarexia (more often called bulimia) is excessive food intake followed by self-induced vomiting or diarrhea.

- Does the desire for a super-thin body contribute to the onset of an eating disorder?

- Does the disorder indicate the presence of a deeper psychological problem?

- What are the physical or neurological effects of anorexia or bulimia?

- Are eating disorders more frequent among certain groups, such as fashion models, athletes, or gay men?

- Do svelte figures on television and in magazine ads contribute to eating disorders?

- What are other factors that contribute?

- You may also want to consider prevention or treatment programs.

Background and Statistics

Diagnostic and Statistical Manual of Mental Disorders: DSM-IV

Eating Disorders: A Reference Sourcebook

Eating Disorders: Opposing Viewpoints

Focus on Eating Disorders: A Reference Handbook

CQ Researcher (online version, *CQ Library,* also available)—*Eating Disorders*

Encyclopedia of Nutrition and Good Health

The Library Catalog

Eating Disorders; Anorexia; Bulimia

Magazines and Newspapers

Medical databases will have good articles containing research results.

CINAHL

MEDLINE—igm.nlm.nih.gov (for information from a professional's viewpoint)

You may also try general and educational databases, such as

PERIODICAL ABSTRACTS

ELECTRIC LIBRARY (for journal articles and transcripts of TV and radio shows)

ERIC—ericir.syr.edu/Eric. Use ERIC especially if you want information on eating disorders on school campuses (college, high school, etc.) and about adolescents and athletes.

Internet

Look for sites sponsored by a medical profession, national support group, or university, such as the following:

Center for Eating Disorders—www.eatingdisorder.org (for news, facts, and discussion)

The National Institute of Mental Health—www.nimh.nih.gov. Search for research and reports.

National Association of Anorexia Nervosa and Associated Disorders—www.anad .org (for definitions, referrals, and therapies)

You will find many sites advertising treatment programs or put together by patients who want to reach out to friends. Although they may have good information, be sure that you evaluate them carefully.

Agencies to Contact

National Association of Anorexia Nervosa and Associated Disorders, Box 7, Highland Park, IL 60035, 847-831-3438

Related Jumpstarts

See Alternative Medicine; Criminal Psychology

34 EDUCATING HOMELESS CHILDREN

Search Terms

(School or Educat?) and Children and Homeless

Head Start

Homeless and (Children or Youth)

Illiteracy and Homelessness

McKinney Act (60 U.S.L.W. 2807, *Lampkins* v. *D.C.*)

Migrant Children

Food for Thought

This serious problem can be broad or local. If you decide to write about schooling homeless children in your city, local resources will be your best sources of information. Try your local newspaper, local school district, and family shelters. Take a look at laws passed to ensure that all children get proper schooling. Nutrition, health, and other issues enter into this "educational" process. How do the schools identify and help these students—particularly because they are so migratory? What about dropout rates?

Background and Statistics

American Homelessness [Contemporary World Issues Series]

Education [Information Plus Series]

Encyclopedia of Social Work

Homeless Children and Youth

The State of America's Children Yearbook

The Library Catalog

Homeless children—Education; Homeless Youth—Education; Homeless Students

Magazines and Newspapers

Even if you are researching local information, you still may want to look at other areas of the country to see what programs and laws they may have to help educate these children. Use any general, educational, or newspaper index, such as

PERIODICAL ABSTRACTS. Look at the current and past year.

Newspapers online at www.usanewspapers.com or www.ecola.com/news/press

ERIC—ericir.syr.edu/Eric

Internet

U.S. Congress—thomas.loc.gov. Take a look in the *Congressional Record* for the congressional conversations taking place on this topic.

National Coalition for the Homeless—nch.ari.net. Read about the Educational Rights project.

Megalaw—www.megalaw.com (to locate laws and cases by state; also includes federal law)

Cornell Law School—www.law.cornell.edu (for state statutes by broad topic or by state)

Agencies to Contact

This is a great topic for a telephone interview. Contact a local shelter, such as the Salvation Army Family Center, and ask the staff about arrangements for the schooling of the children who reside there. Also, contact the principal (or assistant principal) of an inner-city school. Also try the following:

National Coalition for the Homeless, 1012 Fourteenth St., NW, #600, Washington, DC 20005-3410, 202-737-6444, nch@ari.net

Related Jumpstarts

See English as America's Official Language; The Homeless

35 ELECTION REFORM

Search Terms

Election Reform
Electoral College
Election Reform Act
McConnell-Torricelli Election Reform Act

Voting Machines
Internet Voting
Voter Disenfranchise?

Food for Thought

In 2000, George W. Bush, Jr. won the presidential election, even though he had lost the popular vote by 550,000 votes. This was because, in the United States, the president and vice-president are not elected by popular vote but by votes in the Electoral College: 270 votes were required to win, and Bush won 271. Throughout the United States, some counties were using punch card ballots that many voters found difficult to read, whereas other counties were voting by more technologically sophisticated methods. In Florida (where the vote was very close), many voters did not punch their cards accurately, so their ballots were disqualified. Some African Americans and members of other ethnic and racial groups reported being discouraged from voting or even being turned away at the polls. People were also discovering that many ballots, such as absentee votes, do not get counted until after election results are announced. These events caused many people to question the way the United States runs its elections. Consider the following issues:

- ⅄ Why was the Electoral College created, and what impact has it had on previous presidential elections? Is it time to establish a new system using popular votes rather than the electoral college?

- ⅄ Why do so many states and counties use punch card ballots? What alternatives are there, and how can they be funded? Is the solution a matter of money and technology?

- ⅄ Is Internet voting feasible and secure? What are the issues involved in online voting?

Background and Statistics

Campaign and Election Reform: A Reference Handbook

CQ Researcher (online version, *CQ Library*, also available)—*Electoral College; election reform*

Issues & Controversies on File (online version, *Facts.com*, also available)—*Electoral College; election reform*

World Almanac

The Library Catalog

Election law—United States; Electoral College; voting machines—standards; punch card systems—ballots; Afro-Americans—suffrage.

Magazines and Newspapers

Try any general database or newspaper, searching with the following terms: *election reform; Electoral College; voter disenfranchisement; vot? and (African Americans or rac?); voting machines;* and *Election Reform Act.*

ACADEMIC INDEX
PERIODICAL ABSTRACTS
EBSCO*HOST*
ELECTRIC LIBRARY
WASHINGTON POST INDEX or any newspaper index
NATIONAL NEWSPAPERS ABSTRACTS
WESTLAW

Internet

The Voting Integrity Project—www.voting-integrity.org. This is a nonpartisan citizens' watchdog group for U.S. election law reform and voter fraud eradication.

Citizens for True Democracy—www.truedemocracy.org. This group is dedicated to improving the fairness of elections through improving voter turnout, abolishing the Electoral College, and campaign finance reform.

National Archives and Records Administration: U.S. Electoral College—www.nara.gov/fedreg/elctcoll. This is an official U.S. government site; it provides background information on the make-up of and laws governing the Electoral College.

Federal Election Commission—www.fec.gov. Learn more about the American election process. Covers topics from Electoral College to campaign finance.

Also go to Yahoo.com and type in *election reform* and *Electoral College* under the U.S. government category. If you do not specify U.S. on the Internet, you may be led to pages on election reform in other countries.

Agencies to Contact

League of Women Voters, 1730 M. Street NW, Suite 100, Washington, DC 20036-4508, 202-429-1965, www.lwv.org. This is a nonpartisan organization devoted to promoting the electoral process. Also check their Web site at www.lwv.org.

Related Jumpstarts

See Campaign Finance Reform; Term Limits

36 → ELECTRONIC COPYRIGHT

Search Terms

Cybercopyright

Intellectual Property

Digital Millennium Copyright Act

Piracy

Internet and (Copyright or Piracy)

Napster

MP3

Tasini v. *The New York Times*

Food for Thought

Copyright laws are intended to balance the rights of authors with the needs of the public for information and ideas. The ease of reproduction and access to the Internet have altered the needs for copyright protection.

- ⋏ The Internet: It's so easy to copy information, a picture, or a Web site and claim it as your own. What are the author's rights?

- ⋏ Copying movies and CDs: If you own a copy, do you have the right to copy it? To share it?

- ⋏ Who owns ideas? Can you copyright them?

- ⋏ Learn about *The White Paper* (online at www.uspto.gov/web/offices/com/doc /ipnii) by the Information Infrastructure Task Force. It explains how intellectual property law applies in cyberspace.

Background and Statistics

The Copyright Handbook: How to Protect & Use Written Works

Copyright Primer for Librarians & Educators

CQ Researcher (online version, *CQ Library*, also available)—*Copyright*

The Library Catalog

Copyright; Data Protection; Intellectual Property; Copyright and Electronic Data Processing; Copyright—Electronic Information Resources

Magazines and Newspapers

Be sure to do a subject search rather than a keyword search or you will be overwhelmed with irrelevant results. Use any general, business, or newspaper index, including

PERIODICAL ABSTRACTS

WASHINGTON POST or another newspaper

COMPUTER SELECT—*Piracy, Patent/Copyright Issue*

ABI INFORM (for a business point of view)

Internet

U.S. Congress—thomas.loc.gov (for legislation)

Association of Research Libraries—www.arl.org/info/frn/copy/copytoc.html (for laws and documents)

University of Texas—www.utsystem.edu/OGC/IntellectualProperty/faculty.htm (for copyright law in the electronic environment)

Stanford University—fairuse.stanford.edu (for copyright and fair use statutes, cases, and Web sites)

National Writers Union—www.nwu.org. Check their Publication Rights Clearinghouse.

Intellectual Property and the National Information Infrastructure—www.uspto.gov/web/offices/com/doc/ipnii (for *The White Paper*)

Agencies to Contact

Creative Incentive Coalition, 1001 G St. NW, Suite 900 East, Washington, DC 10001, 202-393-1010, www.cic.org/

Digital Future Coalition, PO Box 7679, Washington, DC 20004, 202-628-6048, dfc@dfc.org

Related Jumpstarts

See Honor System in Colleges; Tort Reform

37 → EMERGING INFECTIOUS DISEASES

Search Terms

AIDS and Infectious Diseases (like TB)

Drug Resistan? (Resistance, Resistant)

Emerging Infectious Disease

Global Climate Change and Disease

Outbreak or Plague

Tuberculosis, Ebola, Hantavirus, etc.

Zoonoses or Zoonotic

Food for Thought

The problem with new strains of old diseases, such as tuberculosis, is that the old medicines are no longer effective. The diseases have become drug resistant, so you might use *drug resistan?* as part of your search. How can this problem be approached? What research is being done?

You might select a specific disease to research, such as Ebola virus or the new strains of mycobacterium, tuberculosis, or Hantavirus. If you choose AIDS, you may be overwhelmed by the amount of information you find; be sure to limit your research to a certain aspect of the disease.

Zoonotic diseases are those that can be transmitted between animals and people. Hantavirus comes from rodents; Ebola from monkeys. Many others are airborne, like tuberculosis. Some of these diseases are brought to the United States by travelers. Also, we no longer isolate the ill. Should we?

Background and Statistics

Contagious and Non-Infectious Diseases Sourcebook

CQ Researcher (online version, *CQ Library*, also available)—*Infectious Disease*

Epidemics: Opposing Viewpoints

Health [Information Plus Series]

State of the World

Year Book of Infectious Disease

The Library Catalog

Epidemiology; Infectious Disease; Communicable Diseases. Subject keyword won't always get every book. Try *emerging disease, drug resistant,* or any specific disease.

The Hot Zone and *The Coming Plague* are great books on this topic, as is the movie *Outbreak.*

Magazines and Newspapers

Medical databases are your best bet:

MEDLINE—igm.nlm.nih.gov/

HEALTH SOURCE PLUS

CINAHL

PERIODICAL ABSTRACTS (for non-medical journal and newspaper articles)

Internet

World Health Organization and The Centers for Disease Control—www.who.int. Covers disease outbreaks and eradication efforts, some in audio and video formats.

Emerging Infectious Disease—www.cdc.gov/ncidod/eid/index.htm. This is an online journal including news, research, and commentary, from the Centers for Disease Control.

MMWR—www.cdc.gov/mmwr. This is an online journal containing morbidity and mortality figures; good for statistics.

Related Jumpstarts

See Cloning and Genetic Research; FDA and Medicine Approval

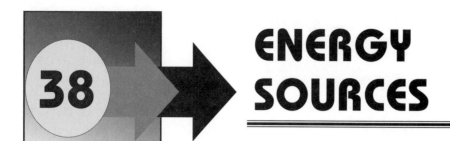

ENERGY SOURCES

Search Terms

Energy Policy Act

Renewable Energy

Deregulation

Energy Shortages

Power Supply

Alternative Energy Sources, such as Coal

Geothermal Hydrogen

Hydropower Methanol

Natural Gas

Nuclear Power

Oil

Solar Energy

Wind Power

Food for Thought

Is oil the best source of energy for now? For the future? Should research funds be spent on finding more oil, finding better ways to use it, or developing other sources of energy altogether? You might want to compare the benefits and disadvantages of oil with those of other energy sources. Which is the most efficient? Most renewable? Least expensive? Consider cost, efficiency, and supply.

Many states are trying or considering deregulating utility companies and allowing consumers to shop for the best rates. In California this has resulted in massive energy shortages. Is deregulation a good idea? Are safeguards needed to protect the consumer? To ensure a reasonable profit for the energy companies?

Background and Statistics

Almanac of Renewable Energy (for basic facts)

CQ Researcher (online version, *CQ Library,* also available)—*Energy Resources*

Energy [Information Plus Series]

Energy Handbook

Issues & Controversies on File (online version, *Facts.com,* also available)—*Energy*

Renewable Energy (for a scientific approach)

United States Energy Atlas (for locations of energy sources)

The Library Catalog

Renewable energy sources; Power resources; Electric Utilities—Deregulation; Energy Development; Energy Policy; Energy Conservation; Energy Consumption

Magazines and Newspapers

Use any general, business, or newspaper index, including

ELECTRIC LIBRARY—*Solar Energy; Nuclear Power; Fossil Fuel*

PERIODICAL ABSTRACTS—*Alternative Energy; Alternative Fuel;* specific fuel

ABI INFORM—*Alternative Energy Sources,* or individual energy sources

Internet

Search *Alternative Energy* or *Deregulation,* or try the following Web sites:

Center for Renewable Energy & Sustainable Technology—solstice.crest.org:80. Covers hydrogen, geothermal energy, and wind and solar energy. Includes companies working with these energy forms.

Department of Energy—www.eren.doe.gov (for federal research on energy sources and deregulation)

Environmental News Network—www.enn.com. Contains environmental news and information from around the world.

Deregulation.com—www.deregulation.com/index.html (for daily news and state deregulation activity)

Agencies to Contact

Department of Energy, Energy Efficiency & Renewable Energy, 1000 Independence Ave. SW, #6C016, Washington, DC 20585, 1-800-363-3732, energyinfo@delphi .com

Center for Renewable Energy & Sustainable Technology, content@solstice.crest .org

Related Jumpstarts

See Alternative Energy; Greenhouse Effect

ENGLISH AS AMERICA'S OFFICIAL LANGUAGE

Search Terms

Bilingual Education

English Only

Language Policy—United States

Official English

Food for Thought

Most countries have an official language. You may be surprised to find that the United States does not. The question is, should we? What are the pros and cons of having an official language?

- ⋏ Who wants English as our official language? Why?

- ⋏ What are the advantages and disadvantages of making English our official language?

- ⋏ Would minority groups be affected by an English-only law?

- ⋏ What is the history of English-only laws?

- ⋏ Consider the English Language Amendment and states with heavy immigrant populations. What would be the repercussions of passing the amendment?

- ⋏ How would statehood for Puerto Rico affect or be affected by English-only laws?

- ⋏ Some towns have enacted Spanish as an official language. Consider the impact on the English-only movement.

- ⋏ Consider the problems and costs of educating children in languages other than English.

Background and Statistics

CQ Researcher (online version, *CQ Library,* also available)—*Official English*

Culture Wars: Opposing Viewpoints

Education: Opposing Viewpoints

Issues & Controversies on File (online version, *Facts.com*, also available)—*Language and Linguistics*

West's Encyclopedia of American Law—*English Only Laws*

The Library Catalog

Language Policy—United States; English Language—United States; Language and Education

Magazines and Newspapers

Use a general or newspaper index, such as the following:

Newspapers online at www.usanewspapers.com or www.ecola.com/news/press

PERIODICAL ABSTRACTS—*English and Language Policy*

Or try a specialized education or legal database, such as the following:

ERIC—ericir.syr.edu/Eric

WESTLAW (for legal information)

Internet

Pro-English-only: English First Official Home Page—www.englishfirst.org (for legislation, census information, and a student resource)

Pro-English-only: U.S. English—www.us-english.org (for legislation and research)

Anti-English-only: American Civil Liberties Union—www.aclu.org. Search the site for *English language* or *English only.*

Megalaw—www.megalaw.com (to locate laws and cases by state; also includes federal law)

Cornell Law School—www.law.cornell.edu (for state statutes by broad topic or by state)

Agencies to Contact

U.S. English, 1747 Pennsylvania Ave. NW, Suite 1100, Washington, DC 20006, 202-833-0100

American Civil Liberties Union, 132 West 43rd St., New York, NY 10036, 212-944-9800

Related Jumpstarts

See Affirmative Action; Educating Homeless Children; Political Correctness

40 → ETHICS AND ORGAN ALLOCATION

Search Terms

Mickey Mantle

Organ Donor (Card)

Organ Transplantation

Organ? and Allocation and Policy

Transplants and Ethics and (Recipient or Allocation)

United Network for Organ Sharing (UNOS)

Food for Thought

With a shortage of organ donors, and a long list of patients awaiting transplants, fair allocation of organs for transplant is an interesting topic. There is talk of a national recipient list, rather than a local pool. Consider the following issues:

- ⅄ How should the recipients be determined? First come, first served? Need? Proximity? How can this be decided?

- ⅄ What policies do different states have?

- ⅄ Should hospitals "presume consent" if no donor card is signed?

- ⅄ What are the ethics of this problem? Is it fair to give transplants to the rich and important first? To the sickest or the healthiest patients? Or to those for whom it is more likely to work? Who decides? You may want to use the Mickey Mantle case as an example.

Background and Statistics

Biomedical Ethics: Opposing Viewpoints

CQ Researcher (online version, *CQ Library*, also available)—*Organ Transplants*

Encyclopedia of Bioethics

Issues & Controversies on File (online version, *Facts.com,* also available)—*Organ Allocation*

Organ Transplants

The Library Catalog

Organ Procurement; Transplantation of Organs; Organ Transplantation

Magazines and Newspapers

Use any general or medical index. Try a medical database and add *ethics.*

PERIODICAL ABSTRACTS—*Transplants and Ethics*

CINAHL

HEALTH SOURCE PLUS—*Organ and Allocation; Transplantation of Organs; Donation of Organs*

MEDLINE—igm.nlm.nih.gov/

Internet

United Network for Organ Sharing—www.unos.org (for statistics and other resources)

U.S. Congress—thomas.loc.gov. Check the *Congressional Record* to see what is being said about this issue.

Transplant Recipients Organization—www.trioweb.org (for legislation, online newsletter, and support for those needing organ donations)

Megalaw—www.megalaw.com (to locate laws and cases by state; also includes federal law)

Cornell Law School—www.law.cornell.edu (for state statutes by broad topic or by state)

Agencies to Contact

Transplant Recipients (TRIIO), 1735 I St. NW, Washington, DC 20006

United Network for Organ Sharing (UNOS), 1100 Boulder Parkway, Suite 500, Richmond, VA 23225

Related Jumpstarts

See Cloning and Genetic Research; FDA and Medicine Approval

41 → ETHICS OF POLITICAL LEADERS

Search Terms

Character

Ethics

House Ethics Committee

Political Corruption

Food for Thought

The pervasiveness of political corruption has become disheartening. President Clinton was caught in the act of lying; congressional leaders have admitted to philandering; local politicians have been convicted of taking bribes. There are many ways to look at this problem.

- Is unethical behavior in politicians a new phenomenon? Find historical examples, if any.

- Are people in general less ethical now, or is the press more inclined to ferret out indiscretions?

- Is corruption peculiar to politicians and others in power?

- Does private infidelity or dishonesty mean a politician is less able? Are independent counsels on political witch hunts or unbiased fact-finding missions?

There is so much information available on this topic that you will be able to handle it better if you limit it by case or a single person or act.

Background and Statistics

CQ Researcher (online version, *CQ Library*, also available)—*Ethics in Government*

Gallup Poll—Moral Values

Issues & Controversies on File (online version, *Fact.com*, also available)—*Politics and Political Reform*

The People, the Press and Politics

Political Scandals: Opposing Viewpoints

Shadow: Five Presidents and the Legacy of Watergate

Presidential Scandals

The Library Catalog

Political Ethics—United States; Political Corruption—United States: Whitewater Inquiry 1993; Corruption (in Politics)

Magazines and Newspapers

Try a general, business, or legal index, such as

ABI INFORM—*Political Ethics*

ELECTRIC LIBRARY (for journal articles and transcripts of TV and radio shows)

PERIODICAL ABSTRACTS

WESTLAW

Internet

Americans against Political Corruption—www.pirg.org/demos/cfr/index.htm (for statistics and ongoing efforts to separate money from politics; state and federal news)

United States Senate—www.senate.gov/committees/index.cfm. Choose Committees, then Select Committee on Ethics.

United States House of Representatives—www.house.gov/reform. Covers Committee on Government Reform, with research and legislation.

Agencies to Contact

Americans Against Political Corruption, 218 D St. SE, 2nd Floor, Washington, DC 20003, 202-546-9707, cressman@essential.org

Related Jumpstarts

See Athletes as Role Models; Honor System in Colleges; Term Limits

ETHNIC CLEANSING

42

Search Terms

(Bosnia or Kosovo) and Yugoslavia

Ethnic Cleansing

Ethnic Relations

Genocide

Holocaust

Human Rights Violations

Rwanda

Food for Thought

The Romans attempted it with the Christians; European explorers wiped out native tribes; Hitler tried it with the Holocaust. Ethnic cleansing is the systematic and planned extermination of an entire national, political, racial, or ethnic group. Should such actions be punished? Who should decide? Consider a modern example, such as Bosnia, Kosovo, Rwanda, or Palestine. The afflicted group is often not able to defend itself. What is the responsibility of a more powerful nation when there is an apparent abuse of power? Or would the world be better off without certain groups? If you take that approach, be sure to read the jumpstart on *Political Correctness*.

Background and Statistics

Atlas of the Holocaust

CQ Researcher (online version, *CQ Library*, also available)—*Human Rights; War Crimes*

Encyclopedia of Genocide

Human Rights: A Reference Handbook

Issues & Controversies on File (online version, *Facts.com*, also available)—*Ethnic Cleansing*

Widening Circle of Genocide

Magazines and Newspapers

Use any general or newspaper index, such as

ELECTRIC LIBRARY (for journal articles and transcripts of television and radio shows)

Newspapers online at www.usanewspapers.com or www.ecola.com/news/press

PERIODICAL ABSTRACTS

WASHINGTON POST or your local newspaper

Internet

Amnesty International—www.amnesty.org. (for news releases, lobbying efforts, and an annual report)

Human Rights Education Association—www.human-rights.net. Search for news and reports.

Web Genocide Documentation Centre—www.ess.uwe.ac.uk/genocide.htm (for articles; timelines; some original sources for many instances of genocide, including Cambodia, Rwanda, Kosovo, and the Third Reich)

Agencies to Contact

Institute for the Study of Genocide, John Jay College of Criminal Justice, 899 10th Ave., Room 325, New York, NY 10019, 212-237-8334

Amnesty International, 322 8th Ave., New York, NY 10001, 212-807-8400, admin-us@aiusa.org

Related Jumpstarts

See Child Labor; Human Rights of Prisoners; Police Brutality

43 → FDA AND MEDICINE APPROVAL

Search Terms

> Food and Drug Administration
>
> Drug Trials and Approvals
>
> AIDS and FDA
>
> FDA and Approval
>
> FDA Regulations
>
> Clinical Trials

Food for Thought

An argument used by those who are ill, particularly AIDS victims, is that medicine takes too long to be approved for human use. Many drugs are used in other parts of the world for years before being approved in the United States. Although this keeps inappropriate drugs off the market (consider the thalidomide babies), it also results in desperate people traveling to other countries for their treatment.

Read a little on this topic before you begin selecting sources. Newspapers have very good articles for background information. You can contact the FDA, but there is so much available that it is probably unnecessary. You might try to find examples of people who have won the right to use medicines before FDA approval. What about Jeff Getty? Look him up. His is a great example.

Background and Statistics

> *CQ Researcher* (online version, *CQ Library,* also available)—*Medical Research*
>
> *Facts on File*
>
> *Macmillan Health Encyclopedia—Clinical Trials*
>
> *West's Encyclopedia of American Law—Food and Drug Administration*

The Library Catalog

United States—Food and Drug Administration; Drugs—Standards; Drugs—Testing—Law and Legislation.

Much of the available information is in government documents and may require a trip to your local Government Document Depository Library.

Magazines and Newspapers

Any medical database will be your best source:

MEDLINE—igm.nlm.nih.gov. Search *FDA and approval.* This medical database will be very good, but watch for articles that are too difficult.

HEALTH SOURCE PLUS

Any general or newspaper index will also have information, including the following:

PERIODICAL ABSTRACTS

Newspapers online at www.usanewspapers.com or www.ecola.com/news/press

Internet

The Internet is a great place to look for this information. Watch for appropriateness.

Food and Drug Administration—www.fda.gov. Search *FDA regulations and medicine.*

Alliance Pharmaceutical Corporation—www.allp.com/drug_dev.htm. This site explains the process of new drug development and approval.

PharmWeb—www.pharmweb.net (for links to government regulatory agencies around the world)

Related Jumpstarts

See Alternative Medicine; Animal Research; Emerging Infectious Diseases

FITNESS FOR CHILDREN

Search Terms

Children—Exercise

Exercise

Fitness and Children

Sports and Children

Physical Fitness for Children

Youth Risk Behavior Surveillance

Food for Thought

According to recent newspaper articles, children are spending more time in front of the television, the obesity rate is increasing, and schools are cutting back on physical education.

⌃ How physically fit are America's children, and how do they compare with children around the world?

⌃ What are the long-term effects of being unfit as a child? The short-term effects?

⌃ Is it detrimental for children to lift weights, run, and exert themselves the way adults do?

⌃ Team sports versus individual sports: Does one type of sport build more confidence than another?

⌃ Why study martial arts (judo, etc.) or ballet as a child?

Background and Statistics

CQ Researcher (online version, *CQ Library,* also available)—*Children, health and safety*

Sports in the Lives of Children and Adolescents

Trends in the Well-Being of America's Children and Youth

The Library Catalog

Physical Fitness for Children; Physical Fitness for Youth; Sports for Children

Magazines and Newspapers

Use any general, medical, or educational index, such as

PERIODICAL ABSTRACTS—*Children and (exercise, sports, sports injury, sports training, or physical fitness).*

ERIC—ericir.syr.edu/Eric (for articles on fitness in schools)

MEDLINE—igm.nlm.nih.gov

HEALTH SOURCE PLUS

CINAHL

Internet

Nemours Foundation—www.kidshealth.org. Medical experts cover all sorts of children's health issues. Do a search for *fitness.*

The President's Challenge Youth Physical Fitness Program—www.indiana.edu /~preschal. Describes the program, with links to other fitness sites.

National Center for Disease Prevention and Health—www.cdc.gov/nccdphp /dnpa (for nutrition and physical activity; includes statistics, reports, and projects)

Related Jumpstarts

See Athletes as Role Models; Sports and Lifelong Benefits

45 ➤ FLEXIBLE WORK SCHEDULES

Search Terms

Alternative Work Pattern

Telecommuting

Job Sharing

Part-Time Employment

Flextime or Flexible (working) Hours

Labor Relations

(Costs or Benefits) and Job Sharing

Food for Thought

With the changing family, flexible schedules may make it possible, or at least easier, for some people to work. Flexible work schedules can include flextime (working four 10-hour days instead of five 8-hour days, for example); job sharing (two people working half time to fill one full-time position); or telecommuting (working from home and staying in touch electronically and via telephone).

- Should companies provide flexible work schedules to already-established employees? Would it be a worthwhile benefit?

- Does job sharing cost the company more money than hiring one person to do a job? What are the costs involved (benefits, training, etc.)?

- Do employees on flexible scheduling give as much to the organization as regular employees? If not, do they give more or less?

- Telecommuting is a type of flexible schedule. When is it a viable option?

Background and Statistics

Encyclopedia of Career Change and Work Issues

Into the Third Century [Information Plus Series]

Women in the Workplace

Women's Changing Role [Information Plus Series]

The Library Catalog

Women—Employment; Hours of Labor, Flexible

Magazines and Newspapers

Use any newspaper, business, or general index, such as

ABI INFORM

PERIODICAL ABSTRACTS

WASHINGTON POST or your local newspaper

Newspapers online at www.usanewspapers.com or www.ecola.com/news/press

Internet

U.S. Congress—thomas.loc.gov (for laws)

U.S. Department of Labor—www.dol.gov (for statistics, laws, and programs)

U. S. Office of Personnel Management—www.opm.gov/ocp/aws—*Handbook on Alternative Work Schedules*

Megalaw—www.megalaw.com (to locate laws and cases by state; also includes federal law)

Cornell Law School—www.law.cornell.edu (for state statutes by broad topic or by state)

Related Jumpstarts

See Child Care; Dual Career Families

FOOD SAFETY

46

Search Terms

Antibiotics and Feed

Delaney Clause

Food and Drug Administration

Food Labeling

Food Poisoning, E coli, Salmonella, etc.

Food Safety

Irradiation/Radiation Preservation

Mad Cow Disease/Creultzfeldt-Jakob Syndrome/Bovine Spongiform Encephalopathy

Food for Thought

Is our food safe to eat?

⅄ Occasional outbreaks of food-related illness are reported in the news, such as Mad Cow Disease, food poisoning, or tainted strawberries.

⅄ New techniques such as irradiated food could have unknown consequences.

⅄ Herbal supplements do not currently have standardized quantities or purity standards.

⅄ Is it healthier to eat organic foods rather than take a chance on pesticide residue?

⅄ Do antibiotics in animal feeds affect human health?

There are many aspects to consider with this topic. You might look at just one area thoroughly or cover several of them as a broader topic.

Background and Statistics

CQ Researcher (online version, *CQ Library*, also available)—*Food and Nutrition*

Facts on File

Food and Animal Borne Diseases

Issues & Controversies on File (online version, *Facts.com*, also available)—*Food Safety*

Nutrition [Information Plus Series]

Silent Spring

The Library Catalog

Foodborne Diseases; Food Handling

Magazines and Newspapers

Try any medical, general, or newspaper index, including the following:

PERIODICAL ABSTRACTS

Newspapers online at www.usanewspapers.com or www.ecola.com/news/press

WASHINGTON POST or your local newspaper

MEDLINE—igm.nlm.nih.org

HEALTH SOURCE PLUS—*Radiation Preservation of Food*

Internet

U.S. Food and Drug Administration—vm.cfsan.fda.gov/list.html

Center for Food Safety and Applied Nutrition—www.FoodSafety.gov. This is a gateway to government food safety information.

U. S. Department of Agriculture—www.fsis.usda.gov (for the food safety and inspection service)

Natural Resources Defense Council—www.nrdc.org (for water safety)

Agencies to Contact

Center for Food Safety & Applied Nutrition, 200 C St. NW, Washington, DC 20204

U.S. Food & Drug Administration, 5600 Fishers Lane, Rockville, MD 20857-0001, 1-888-INFOFDA

Related Jumpstarts

See Cloning and Genetic Research; FDA and Medicine Approval

GAMBLING AS A MORAL ISSUE

Search Terms

Gambling—Social Conditions

Compulsive Gambling

Gambling and Moral?

Public Opinion and Gambling

Gambling and Organized Crime

Compulsive Gambling and Impact

Food for Thought

Are Americans changing their minds about the ethics or morals of gambling? We see a dramatic increase in the number of state lotteries and casinos. Ten years ago Las Vegas was for grown-ups. Today most visitors to Las Vegas are families, and children gamble for prizes at arcades. Consider some of the following questions:

- Who, exactly, is doing the gambling? Is it effectively a "tax" against the poor?

- Now that gambling is easily accessible, are there more compulsive gamblers? Does gambling increase poverty?

- How does gambling affect the individual gambler and his or her family?

- Does it encourage organized crime?

- Does the prevalence of gambling reflect lower moral standards?

- Have state lotteries affected attitudes about gambling?

- Are religious institutions involved in this issue? Do they promote (with Bingo nights, for example) or discourage gambling?

Background and Statistics

A Matter of Fact. Contains good quotes with statistics.

CQ Researcher (online version, *CQ Library,* also available)—*Gambling*

Legalized Gambling [Contemporary World Issues Series]

Gambling [Information Plus Series]

The Gallup Poll

The Library Catalog

Gambling; Compulsive Gambling; Legalized Gambling

Magazines and Newspapers

Use the listed keywords to search for articles in newspapers and journals. Use any general or newspaper index, including

Newspapers online at www.usanewspapers.com or www.ecola.com/news/press

PERIODICAL ABSTRACTS. This is your best source.

Internet

The Internet is an interesting place to look for this topic, but please evaluate carefully what you find. On the Internet, everyone has access to post their opinion, and many sites lack the authority you would need for a bona fide research paper.

North American Association of State and Provincial Lotteries (NASPL)—www.naspl.org /research.html (for links to research on gambling)

University of Nevada Reno—www.unr.edu/gaming/frame.htm—Institute for the Study of Gambling and Commercial Gaming.

European Association for the Study of Gambling—www.easg.org.
Go to *Publications.*

National Gambling Impact Study Commission—www.ngisc.gov. The Commission's research and the final report are online.

Agencies to Contact

National Gambling Impact Study Commission, 800 N. Capitol St. NW, Suite 450, Washington, DC 20002, 202-523-8217

Related Jumpstarts

See State Lotteries

48 → GANGS

Search Terms

Gangs and Ethnicity (Name a Group)

Gangs and Prevention

Gangs and Violence

Gangs and Schools

Gangs and Peer Pressure

Food for Thought

Limit your search or you will find too much information. Following are some possible topics:

- Gangs: urban or rural phenomenon, or both?
- Who joins gangs?
- Gangs and rap singers
- Government anti-gang programs
- What kinds of violence do they commit?
- Gangs in schools
- Gang initiation ceremonies
- Evolution of gangs
- Peer pressure and gangs
- Gang identification: colors, hand signs, graffiti

Background and Statistics

CQ Researcher (online version, *CQ Library*, also available)

Gangs: Opposing Viewpoints

Issues & Controversies on File (online version, *Facts.com*, also available)

Street Gang Awareness

The Library Catalog

Gangs; School Violence; Juvenile Delinquency

Magazines and Newspapers

Use any educational, general, or newspaper index, including

PERIODICAL ABSTRACTS. Try searching *Gangs* as a subject, and other words as keywords.

Your local newspaper. Use this especially for local gangs.

ERIC—ericir.syr.edu/Eric—*Gangs and Schools*

Internet

Many Web sites are available; look especially for credentialed sites created by national support groups and local, state, and federal government agencies.

U.S. Department of Justice—www.usdoj.gov (for youth violence)

Juvenile Justice Clearinghouse—www.criminology.fsu.edu/jjclearinghouse/about.html (from Florida State University)

Office of Juvenile Justice and Delinquency Prevention—ojjdp.ncjrs.org (for statistics, gang signs and dress, case flow through the juvenile justice system)

Agencies to Contact

Juvenile Justice Clearing House, 1-800-638-8736

Related Jumpstarts

See Cults; Curfews; Youth Crime

GENDER DIFFERENCES: ENVIRONMENTAL OR GENETIC?

Search Terms

Gender Differences

Sex Differences

Sex Roles

Sexes and (Salary or Suicide or ??)

Food for Thought

Try to look for the facts. First, which gender differences are real? Which are influenced by societal expectations? You may find information on teacher bias in schools, where girls receive less attention than boys, and on society's unfair expectations of boys, who supposedly are not allowed to show emotion. A recent study showed that when people are reminded of stereotypes before a test (girls cannot do math, white boys cannot jump) they tend to meet those stereotypes. What are ways in which males or females are affected by gender differences (pay, learning, stress, violence)? Do we perceive the roles of men and women in the same way we did a generation ago? Can we take advantage of gender differences to improve society? There have been many studies on this topic. Try to locate them.

Background and Statistics

CQ Researcher (online version, *CQ Library*, also available)

Encyclopedia of Psychology

Handbook of Child Psychology

Inequality: Opposing Viewpoints in Social Problems

Male/Female Roles: Opposing Viewpoints

Oxford Companion to the Mind

Women's Changing Role [Information Plus Series]

Statistical Handbook on Women in America

The Library Catalog

Sex Differences; Sex Differences (psychology)

Magazines and Newspapers

Medical and education databases are your best sources:

CINAHL—*Sex factors*

HEALTH SOURCE PLUS—*Sex differences*

ERIC—ericir.syr.edu/Eric—*Sex differences; gender issues*

PERIODICAL ABSTRACTS—*Sexes and (academic achievement, sports, etc.); gender differences.*

Internet

Although there is plenty of information, both the words *gender* and *sex* can bring up undesirable sites. Use the sites recommended below, or use very specific search terms; for example, *sex differences and communication; and hearing; and brain size.* Try both *sex differences* and *gender differences.*

Amoeba Web, provided by Vanguard University of Southern California—www.sccu.edu/psychology/webgender.html (for psychological differences)

Educational Testing Service—www.ets.org. Examines gender differences on standardized tests.

National Institutes of Health—www.nida.nih.gov/WHGD/WHGDHome.html (for women's health and gender differences)

Agencies to Contact

National Center for Educational Statistics, U. S. Department of Education, Capitol Place, 555 New Jersey Ave. NW, Washington, DC 20208, 202-219-1828

Related Jumpstarts

See Affirmative Action; Glass Ceiling; Women's Athletics

50 → GLASS CEILING

Search Terms

Glass Ceiling

Women—Employment

Women and Benefits

Lynn Martin—Glass Ceiling Commission Chairperson

Food for Thought

- ⅄ As employees climb the corporate ladder, is there an invisible glass ceiling beyond which certain employees, because of gender, cannot advance?

- ⅄ When women are promoted, do they receive the same benefits and salary for equal work?

- ⅄ Is inequity a result of bias, or are women responsible for building a glass ceiling by choosing more nurturing jobs rather than those that pay better?

- ⅄ Is there really a glass ceiling? Find proof, if you can, in salary schedules and listings of upper management company personnel. If you believe there is a glass ceiling, what are the possible solutions?

Background and Statistics

CQ Researcher (online version, *CQ Library,* also available)

Encyclopedia of Career Change and Work Issues—Careers

Feminism: Opposing Viewpoints

The Legal Rights of Women

Women's Changing Role

Women's Rights on Trial

Working Women: Opposing Viewpoints

The Library Catalog

Women Executives; Sex Discrimination in Employment; Sex Discrimination Against Women.

Also try subject keyword searching for *Glass Ceiling; Women Employment.*

There are plenty of books on this topic. Watch for currency.

Magazines and Newspapers

Try a business or general index such as the following:

ABI INFORM. This business database is the best possible place for this research. You can probably just use ABI and find more than enough information for a short paper.

PERIODICAL ABSTRACTS

Internet

There are many Web pages that argue that there is a glass ceiling. Following are examples:

U.S. Department of Labor—www.dol.gov. Search the site for *glass ceiling, economic equity,* and other appropriate search terms.

U.S. Congress—thomas.loc.gov (for legislation and discussion by Congress)

National Organization for Women—www.now.org (for information on economic equity)

Related Jumpstarts

See Affirmative Action; Gender Differences

51 GREEN COMPANIES

Search Terms

Energy Efficiency

Energy Management

Green Wall

Valdez Principles

Environmentalism

Food for Thought

Some companies are making heroic efforts to promote corporate environmental responsibility. In other companies, there is a "green wall" erected between the environmentalists and the rest of the company. Consider specific, higher risk industries, such as chemical production or logging.

- Is environmentalism cost-effective?
- Should cost-effectiveness be a deciding factor in choosing environmental approaches?
- Is it worth losing hundreds of jobs to save one species from extinction?
- Are we damaging the environment beyond repair?

Consider short-term and long-term effects. You might want to find specific cases.

Background and Statistics

Environmental Almanac

Encyclopedia of the Environment

Conservation & Environmentalism

Greening of American Business

The Library Catalog

Green Movement; Environmental Policy—United States; Environmental Health; Environmental Protection; Human Ecology; Business Enterprises—United States—Environmental Aspects; Social Responsibility of Business; United States—Industries—Environmental Aspects; Green Marketing

Magazines and Newspapers

Use any business or general database, including

ABI INFORM—*energy efficiency; energy management.* As a keyword search, try *green wall.*

PERIODICAL ABSTRACTS—*Corporate responsibility and environment?* as keyword search.

Internet

If you choose an issue, such as an industry or a company in the news, you can search particular terms. For more general sites, the Internet is not a good source. Try the following site:

Environmental Defense Fund—www.edf.org. This site is more likely to give you the companies that abuse the environment than those that are "green."

Agencies to Contact

Environmental Defense Team, 1875 Connecticut Ave. NW, Suite 1016, Washington, DC 20009

Environmental Defense Fund, 257 Park Ave. S., New York, NY 10010, 1-800-684-3322

Related Jumpstarts

See Energy Sources; Ozone Layer

52 ➤ GREENHOUSE EFFECT

Search Terms

Atmospheric Ozone

Montreal Protocol

Ozone or Ozone Layer

Greenhouse Effect

Rainforest Depletion

Food for Thought

Modern technology is blamed for causing damage to the ozone layer miles above the Earth. Developed nations have agreed to stop producing many offending products but have not convinced developing nations to do the same. Start with the causes of the greenhouse effect.

⌐ How did it come about?

⌐ What can be done to correct it?

⌐ How does it affect us?

⌐ How can individuals help?

Consider researching a single aspect of this enormous problem; for example: "The greenhouse effect is the cause of the warming weather conditions," or "The greenhouse effect will cause universal flooding as the polar ice caps melt."

Background and Statistics

CQ Researcher (online version, *CQ Library*, also available)—*Ozone; Environment*

Encyclopedia of Climate and Weather—Ozone Hole

Gale Encyclopedia of Science—Ozone Layer Depletion

Weather Almanac—Ozone Layer Depletion

The Library Catalog

Ozone Layer Depletion; Atmospheric Ozone; Air—Pollution; Greenhouse Effect; Global Warming

Magazines and Newspapers

Use any health or general index, such as

HEALTH SOURCE PLUS—*Ozone Layer Depletion*

PERIODICAL ABSTRACTS—*Montreal Protocol; Ozone and Environmental Protection*

Internet

Environmental Protection Agency (EPA)—www.epa.gov/docs/ozone (for Ozone depletion laws)

U.S. Department of Energy—www.energy.gov

CIESIN—www.ciesin.org/TG/OZ/oz-home.html (for causes, environmental effects, and policy responses)

Megalaw—www.megalaw.com (to locate laws and cases by state; also includes federal law)

Cornell Law School—www.law.cornell.edu (for state statutes by broad topic or by state)

Agencies to Contact

Committee for the National Interest for the Environment, 1725 K St. NW, Suite 212, Washington, DC 20006, 202-520-5810, cnie@cnie.org, www.cnie.org/nle/air-3.html

Ozone Protection Hotline, 800-296-1996

Related Jumpstarts

See Green Companies; Ozone Layer

53 ➤ GUN CONTROL

Search Terms

Firearms   Handguns
Gun Control   Firearms Laws
Brady (Bill or Law)   Concealed Weapons
Weapons

Food for Thought

Most people have very strong views on gun control, both for and against, and are not willing to consider the opposite point of view. To write a persuasive paper, be sure you research both sides of the issue. For every topic, you can argue better if you know what the other side believes. Following are common arguments about gun control:

➤ Weapons don't kill; people kill.
   The only purpose of a handgun is to shoot someone.

➤ If guns weren't legal, criminals would still find a way to get them.
   Up to 70 percent of guns used by felons are stolen from private homes.

➤ Our constitutional right to bear arms is protected by the Second Amendment.
   The medical cost of gun violence is $4.5 billion per year.

Proposed compromises include waiting periods before purchasing and "smart" guns. You may want to address these.

Background and Statistics

CQ Researcher (online version, *CQ Library*, also available)—*Firearms*

Uniform Crime Reports for the United States (also online at www.fbi.gov/ucr.htm)

Encyclopedia of Crime and Justice—Guns, regulation of Gun Control [Information Plus Series]

Issues & Controversies on File (online version, *Facts.com*, also available)

National Survey of State Laws

Statistical Handbook on Violence in America

West's Encyclopedia of American Law

The Library Catalog

Gun Control; Firearms—Law and Legislation

Magazines and Newspapers

General and newspaper indexes will have plenty of discussion:

ELECTRIC LIBRARY—*Gun Control; Brady Bill*

PERIODICAL ABSTRACTS—*Firearms laws and regulations; National Rifle Association*

Newspapers online at www.usanewspapers.com or www.ecola.com/news/press

Internet

Right to Bear Arms Sites

Potomac Institute—www.potomac-inc.org/index.html (for Second Amendment arguments)

Arms Rights and Liberty—www.rkba.org (for firearms links)

National Rifle Association—www.nraila.org/—Institute for Legislative Action

Gun Control Sites

Handgun Control Organization—www.handguncontrol.org (for politics and press releases)

Unbiased Sites

University of Pittsburgh School of Law—www.jurist.law.pitt.edu/gunlaw.htm. This is a resource for issues on both sides of the controversy.

CNN—www.cnn.com/SPECIALS/1998/schools/gun.control (for state laws)

Bureau of Alcohol, Tobacco and Firearms—www.atf.treas.gov (for regulations and statistics)

For laws, use thomas.loc.gov and search for *firearms safety.*

Megalaw—www.megalaw.com (to locate laws and cases by state; also includes federal law)

Cornell Law School—www.law.cornell.edu (for state statutes by broad topic or by state)

If you use a search engine, the words *Gun Control* will lead you to information against gun control. *Brady Bill* will have more pro-control information.

Agencies to Contact

National Rifle Association, 1600 Rhode Island Ave. NW, Washington, DC 20036, nra-contact@NRA.org

Handgun Control, Inc., 1225 Eye St. NW, Suite 1100, Washington, DC 20005, 202-898-0792

Related Jumpstarts

See School Violence

54 → HAZARDOUS WASTE

Search Terms

Hazardous Waste

Toxic Waste

Nuclear or Radioactive Waste

Medical Waste

Waste Disposal

Food for Thought

Refine your topic to a single small issue within a type of hazardous waste; for example, *disease and medical waste* or *White Sands, NM and nuclear radiation*. Other possible issues are

- ⅄ Nuclear waste: Is the energy produced worth the waste product it creates?

- ⅄ Medical or chemical waste

- ⅄ Contaminated waste sites: Who is responsible for the waste: the government, the current owner of the site, or the owner that produced the contamination?

- ⅄ Household garbage

- ⅄ Superfund

- ⅄ Contaminated water

- ⅄ Effect of hazardous waste on wildlife

- ⅄ Effect of hazardous waste on human health

Background and Statistics

CQ Researcher (online version, *CQ Library,* also available)

Environment [Information Plus Series]

Government Assistance Almanac

Issues & Controversies on File (online version, Facts.com, also available)—Nuclear Waste

Standard Handbook of Hazardous Waste Treatment & Disposal

The Library Catalog

Hazardous Waste; Nuclear Waste. You'll find books, state, and government documents on this topic.

Magazines and Newspapers

Try business, general, or newspaper databases for hazardous waste disposal items:

ABI INFORM

Newspapers online at www.usanewspapers.com or www.ecola.com/news/press

PERIODICAL ABSTRACTS

ELECTRIC LIBRARY for journal articles and transcripts of television and radio shows

For medical waste, or for the effects of hazardous waste on humans, try medical databases:

MEDLINE—igm.nlm.nih.gov

CINAHL

Internet

National Oceanic and Atmospheric Administration—response.restoration.noaa.gov /cpr/wastesites/wastesites.html (for coastal hazardous waste site reviews)

United Nations—www.basel.int (for international treaty on hazardous wastes)

Environmental Protection Agency—www.epa.gov/osw (for identification, legislation, and disposal of hazardous wastes)

Agencies to Contact

Environmental Protection Agency, 401 M St., SW, Washington, DC 20460. Check your local phone book for a regional office.

Related Jumpstarts

See Green Companies; Ozone Layer

55 → HEALTH INSURANCE DEBATE

Search Terms

Health Care Reform

Medical Policy

Kennedy-Kassebaum Health Insurance Reform Bill (1996)

Medicare

HMO

Food for Thought

Many other countries have universal health insurance. Should everyone in the United States be insured? Are there tradeoffs, such as higher taxes, a limited selection of doctors available, or poorer quality of medical care? Consider the health care reform plans.

- ⌐ What would be best, HMOs, PPOs, or an extension of Medicare? Compare them.

- ⌐ Are HMOs infringing on individuals' rights, second guessing doctors, or making decisions based solely on cost?

- ⌐ Would universal health care stifle medical research because it costs too much?

Background and Statistics

CQ Researcher (online version, *CQ Library,* also available)

Health [Information Plus Series]

Health Care in America: Opposing Viewpoints

The Library Catalog

Medical Policy—United States; Insurance, Health; Health Policy; National Health Insurance

There are many government documents on this topic if you have a depository nearby.

Magazines and Newspapers

Use any medical, business, general, or newspaper index, including

ELECTRIC LIBRARY for journal articles and transcripts of TV and radio shows

PERIODICAL ABSTRACTS

WASHINGTON POST for information on Medicaid and government legislation

ABI INFORM

CINAHL

HEALTH SOURCE PLUS

MEDLINE—igm.nlm.nih.org. If you use this database, combine keywords to limit your search.

Internet

There's lots of information on health care reform on the Internet.

National Center for Policy Analysis—www.public-policy.org/~ncpa/pi/health /hedex1.html (for issues and legislation in the United States and elsewhere)

U.S. Congress—thomas.loc.gov. (for laws and debate in Congress)

Physicians for a National Health Care Program—www.pnhp.org (for policies, proposals, bibliography, and information for students)

Agencies to Contact

Health Care Financing Administration, 200 Independence Ave. SW, Washington, DC 20042, 202-690-6113

National Health Policy Forum, 2021 K St. NW, Suite 800, Washington, DC 20201, 202-872-1390

Related Jumpstarts

See FDA and Medicine Approval; Social Security Reform; Tax Reform

56 → THE HOMELESS

Search Terms

Homeless or Homelessness

Housing and Homeless

McKinney Act

Shelters and Homeless

Any of the causes listed below and Homeless

Food for Thought

⅄ Can homelessness be prevented?

⅄ Should panhandling be allowed?

⅄ What is the responsibility of citizens to remedy this problem? What is the responsibility of the government? The private social services agencies?

⅄ Are Americans losing sympathy for the homeless?

⅄ How can citizens help with this problem?

Consider causes, such as lack of affordable housing, drug or alcohol addiction, mental illness, disabilities, lack of employment opportunities, and health issues. You may think of others. What could be done to minimize these problems?

Background and Statistics

CQ Researcher (online version, *CQ Library*, also available)

Homeless in America [Contemporary World Issues]

Historic Documents

Social Welfare [Information Plus Series]

Homeless in America [Information Plus Series]

Homelessness: A Sourcebook

The State of America's Children

The Library Catalog

Homeless Persons

Magazines and Newspapers

Use any general or newspaper index, including

PERIODICAL ABSTRACTS

WASHINGTON POST or your local newspaper (for local homeless issues)

Internet

National Coalition for the Homeless—nch.ari.net (for news alerts, facts, and legislation)

Habitat for Humanity—www.habitat.org. This organization is dedicated to building homes for families and communities in need.

Agencies to Contact

National Coalition for the Homeless, 1012 14th St. NW, #600, Washington, DC 20005-3410, 202-737-6444, nhc@ari.net

Habitat for Humanity, 121 Habitat St., Americus, GA 31709-3498, 912-924-6935, public_info@habitat.org

Related Jumpstarts

See Educating Homeless Children; Hunger in America

57 ➤ HONOR SYSTEM IN COLLEGES

Search Terms

Cheating

Codes of Ethics

Honesty

Honor System

Plagiarism

Academic Integrity

Food for Thought

Term papers are for sale on the Internet. Faculty members are requiring students to submit copies of their information sources to prove that they themselves did the work. It is easier than ever to copy someone else's test by downloading it onto a disk. Has the diminishing moral fiber of the United States made the honor system passé? Is the U.S. public desensitized to the subject of cheating? Does an honor system increase or decrease the chance of cheating? There is an abundance of information on this subject in journals, but not much in books. Many colleges post their honor codes online. You will find some by searching for the college name and *honor* or *integrity.*

The Library Catalog

Cheating (Education); College Students—United States—Conduct of Life

Magazines and Newspapers

Use any education, general, or newspaper index, such as

PERIODICAL ABSTRACTS—*Plagiarism and College*

WASHINGTON POST or your local newspaper

Newspapers online at www.usanewspapers.com or www.ecola.com/news/press

CHRISTIAN SCIENCE MONITOR—www.csmonitor.com. This paper has 15 years archived on the Internet.

ERIC—ericir.syr.edu/Eric. This is the best place to look for information about the honor system in schools.

Internet

Many colleges have their honor policies online. Search using *Honor System; Code of Honor; Academic Integrity.*

Center for Academic Integrity—www.nwu.edu/uacc/cai/main.html (for sharing of ideas for enforcement, sanctions, and prevention)

Dalhousie University Libraries—www.library.dal.ca/killam/instruct/detect.htm (for information on detecting plagiarism)

Agencies to Contact

Center for Academic Ethics, c/o Dr. Arthur Brown, Wayne State University, 311 Education Bldg., Detroit, MI 48202

Related Jumpstarts

See Electronic Copyright; Ethics of Political Leaders

58 → HUMAN RIGHTS OF PRISONERS

Search Terms

Prison Reform

Prisoner or inmate

Inmates' Rights

Prison Conditions

Prison? and (Rights or Privileges)

Food for Thought

First, you will have to focus your topic on prisoners in the United States or those in other countries. This jumpstart concentrates on prisoners in the United States.

⅄ Are prisons too comfortable? Or too dangerous? In your search, much of what you will find will concern prisoners in other countries.

⅄ For certain types of inmates, prisons may be especially dangerous. The young, or those who look young, and the gay may find themselves prey to sexual molesters. People imprisoned for certain types of crimes may be subjected to retaliation in prison. A racial minority may be persecuted. Should these people receive "separate but equal" treatment?

⅄ Should prisoners retain their constitutional rights? Try to identify constitutional rights and compare them with privileges.

⅄ Human rights for prisoners may include religious rights (such as kosher food).

⅄ Are some types of treatment, such as isolation, overcrowding, lack of privacy, or minimal health care, part of the punishment or an abuse of human rights?

Background and Statistics

American Prison System: The Reference Shelf

CQ Researcher (online version, *CQ Library*, also available)

Encyclopedia of Crime and Justice

Issues & Controversies on File (online version, *Facts.com*, also available)

Prisons and Jails [Information Plus Series]

The Library Catalog

Prisons; Prison Reform; Prisons—Education; Prisoners—Civil Rights; Prisoners—Legal Status

Magazines and Newspapers

Use any legal or general index, including

PERIODICAL ABSTRACTS—*Prisons and Human Rights.* Most items will be about foreign prisons; you'll have to weed through them.

Newspapers online at www.usanewspapers.com or www.ecola.com/news/press

WESTLAW (for transcripts of court cases)

Internet

National Criminal Justice Information Center—www.ncjrs.org (for information on prison reform)

Federal Bureau of Prisons—www.bop.gov (for information on inmates' rights)

Amnesty International—www.amnesty.org (for an international point of view)

United Nations Human Rights Website—www.unhchr.ch. Presents a world view.

Related Jumpstarts

See Capital Punishment; Police Brutality

59 → HUNGER IN AMERICA

Search Terms

Hunger and (Your City)

Public Assistance Programs

Food Stamps

Children and Hunger

Hunger and (Nutrition or Health)

Welfare and Hunger

Food for Thought

Although world hunger is often a hot issue, the local hunger problem is often ignored. You may want to limit your search to hunger in your area. If you do so, local resources (telephone interviews, local newspapers, and government agencies) may be your best resources. Your library will have plenty of information on this topic. A good argument might have to do with any of the topics listed under "Search Terms." Be sure to look for statistics for your paper.

Consider the various aspects of the problem.

- Are welfare programs and food stamps helping to alleviate hunger or enabling it by keeping people dependent?

- Are school lunch programs working?

- Many communities have local food pantries. Do they reach those in need?

- Is hunger temporary or a chronic problem for those who come for assistance?

- What are the repercussions of undernourishment for productivity, educational achievement, and crime?

- Can you think of a plan that would help alleviate this problem?

Background and Statistics

CQ Researcher (online version, *CQ Library,* also available)—*Food Supply*

Encyclopedia of Nutrition and Good Health

Encyclopedia of Social Work—Hunger

Matter of Fact—Hunger

Nutrition [Information Plus Series]

Social Welfare [Information Plus Series]

The State of American Children

The Library Catalog

Food Relief: United States, or use subject keyword: *hunger, food supply.* World hunger books will come up along with hunger in America.

Magazines and Newspapers

Use any medical, general, or newspaper index, including

HEALTH SOURCE PLUS—*Hunger and nutrition; welfare; food stamp programs*

PERIODICAL ABSTRACTS

Newspapers online at www.usanewspapers.com

Internet

Congressional Record—thomas.loc.gov. Search for *hunger.* You'll find many entries here.

America's Second Harvest—www.secondharvest.org. Explains who's hungry in America and what you can do to help.

The Salvation Army—www.salvationarmyusa.org. Contains information about disaster relief.

Also search www.metacrawler.com using *hunger America.*

Agencies to Contact

Many agencies and churches provide food to the poor. Try your local Salvation Army, religious institution, or food bank.

Related Jumpstarts

See Educating Homeless Children; The Homeless; World Population and Hunger

60 ➤ ILLEGAL IMMIGRATION

Search Terms

Emigration or Immigration
Green Card
Border Patrols
Federal Aid and Immigrants and Illegal

Work and Illegal and Immigra?
Elian Gonzales
H1B Visas
Illegal Aliens

Food for Thought

This jumpstart is intended to cover both illegal and legal immigration, because many of the resources are the same. However, you should decide which interests you. Is your topic "immigration reform?"

➤ What is the government doing to curtail the illegal entry of aliens into the United States?

➤ Should everyone be allowed to come to the United States? Will they take jobs that are currently unfilled or make it harder for U.S. citizens to find work?

➤ Is H1B, intended to bring in workers in needed fields, being abused by companies looking for those willing to accept lower pay?

➤ Are you interested in the plight of illegal immigrants in the United States?

➤ Should they be allowed to work?

➤ Should they be eligible for social services such as health care and food stamps?

➤ Are company owners using them so they can pay lower wages?

➤ Are they being abused, working long hours, and being kept in substandard accommodations because they have no recourse?

➤ Even if that is true, are they better off than they would be in their native countries?

➤ Should their children be educated in our school systems?

➤ What about child labor?

Consider relevant legislation:

➤ the 1986 Immigration Reform Control Act;

➤ the Asylum & Immigration Act 1996;

↙ Proposition 187 (in California); and

↙ laws regarding school for children of illegal immigrants.

You'll find federal laws in Thomas (see "Internet") or WESTLAW.

Background and Statistics

It's important to try to find statistics to back up your arguments on this topic.

CQ Researcher (online version, *CQ Library,* also available)—*Immigration*

The Guide to American Law—Alien

Immigration: Opposing Viewpoints

Immigration and Illegal Aliens [Information Plus Series]

Issues & Controversies on File (online version, *Facts.com,* also available)—*Public School Funds*

A Matter of Fact—Immigrants; Emigration

Statistical Abstracts of the US—also online at www.census.gov/stat_abstract

West's Encyclopedia of American Law

The Library Catalog

Illegal Aliens – United States; Emigration and Immigration Law

Magazines and Newspapers

Use any general, newspaper, or legal index, including

PERIODICAL ABSTRACTS

Newspapers online at www.usanewspapers.com or www.ecola.com/news/press

WESTLAW

Internet

Immigration and Naturalization Service—www.ins.usdoj.gov/graphics/lawenfor /index.htm (for information on the Border Patrol)

Project USA—www.projectusa.org. This organization would like to stop all immigration.

Library of Congress—thomas.loc.gov (for federal laws)

Agencies to Contact

Immigration and Naturalization Service. Check the telephone book for a local number.

Related Jumpstarts

See English as America's Official Language; Income Gap; World Population and Hunger

61 INCOME GAP

Search Terms

(Income or Wage) Gap and (Women or . . .)

Comparable Worth

Equal Pay Act

Equal Pay for Equal Work

Glass Ceiling (not JUST about income)

Inequality in Earnings

Pay Equity

Wage Differential

Wage Discrimination

Food for Thought

"Income gap" is a hot topic, but what "gap" are we talking about? Once you have decided on the group you want to research, the keywords will be for that group. This is a topic that can be argued from either side. One group deserves to earn the same pay as the other because . . . or it does not, because . . .

Following are some "gaps" from which to select:

⅄ Any ethnic group versus whites

⅄ Executives versus workers

⅄ Women versus men

⅄ Educated versus skilled workers

⅄ Rich versus poor

Statistics will be important to establish your premise. If you can find case examples, they would be even better.

Background and Statistics

CQ Researcher (online version, *CQ Library,* also available)—*Income Inequality*

Handbook of U.S. Labor Statistics

Social Welfare [Information Plus Series]

West's Encyclopedia of American Law—*Comparable Worth*

The Library Catalog

Equal Pay for Equal Work; Women—*Employment; Pay Equity; Discrimination in Employment*

Magazines and Newspapers

Use any business, general, or newspaper index, including

ABI INFORM

PERIODICAL ABSTRACTS

WASHINGTON POST or your local newspaper

Newspapers online at www.usanewspapers.com or www.ecola.com/news/press

Internet

U.S. Department of Labor—www.dol.gov (for statistics and laws)

Center on Budget and Policy Priorities—www.cbpp.org (for analysis of IRS income data, state-by-state income trends)

American Federation of Labor—www.aflcio.org/home.htm. Do a search on *income gap* or *equal pay.*

Agencies to Contact

Urban Institute, 2100 M St. NW, Washington, DC 20037, 202-857-8709, www.urban.org

Center on Budget & Policy Priorities, 820 First St. NE, Suite 510, Washington, DC 20002, 202-408-1080

Related Jumpstarts

See Affirmative Action; Glass Ceiling

MEDIA INFLUENCE ON PUBLIC OPINION

Search Terms

Media or Mass Media

Public Relations

Public Opinion and (Media or Journalism)

Media and Propaganda

Journalism or Journalists

Media and Influence

Food for Thought

Many feel that media influence has become unhealthy; that the media have begun to select the issues Americans consider important rather than the other way around. The competition for speed of news delivery on the Internet and television has increased the pressure to sell information. Keep in mind that you are looking for information in the very same sources you are examining. This may be a good topic for interviews. Consider the following questions:

⅄ What impact has the Internet or television had on public thinking?

⅄ How has the speed of communication affected what people think?

⅄ What about the pressure on the news reporters or anchors? Does it affect ethical behavior?

⅄ How are corporations using advertising to sell a corporate image?

⅄ Does the nightly news influence people to have a particular viewpoint?

⅄ Does the nightly news influence politics?

⅄ In what ways might an advertiser influence the media?

Background and Statistics

Age of Propaganda

American Values

CQ Researcher (online version, *CQ Library*, also available)—*Journalism; talk shows; television; Internet; Political advertising*

Gallup Poll

Issues & Controversies on File (online version, Facts.com, also available)—*Advertising; public opinion; politics; television; Internet*

Mass Media: Opposing Viewpoints

PR: How The Public Relations Industry Writes the News

The Library Catalog

Public Relations; Propaganda; Journalism; Media; Mass Media; Violence as Communication

Magazines and Newspapers

Try any general database or newspaper and use a variety of terms. The newspaper will be a good source to examine. Journals will discuss the issue of media influence.

ACADEMIC INDEX

PERIODICAL ABSTRACTS

NEWSPAPERS ONLINE—www.usanewspapers.com or www.ecola.com/news/press

SIRS GOVERNMENT REPORTER

WASHINGTON POST—www.washingtonpost.com, or any newspaper

Internet

Media Literacy—interact.uoregon.edu/MediaLit/HomePage. This site is concerned with the influence of media in the lives of children and youth.

Media Influence on Children—www.adl.org/what_to_tell/whattotell_media.html. This is the Anti-Defamation League's help for parents on this topic.

Media Literacy Online—interact.uoregon.edu/MediaLit/HomePage

There are many Web sites that tackle this problem. Newspapers and journal articles seem to be the best bet. Try the following words online at www.metacrawler.com: *mass media, public opinion; television influence; public opinion; media influence.*

Agencies to Contact

FAIR (Fairness and Accuracy in Reporting), 130 W. 25th St., New York, NY 10001, www.fair.org

The Media Foundation, 1243 W. 7th Ave., Vancouver, BC V6H1B7, www.adbusters .org/information/foundation/

Related Jumpstarts

See Political Correctness

63 MEDICINAL USES OF MARIJUANA

Search Terms

Cannabis

Marijuana and Medicinal Use

California Proposition 215

Arizona Proposition 200

Food for Thought

When California, Colorado, and Arizona offered voters a chance to legalize marijuana for medical purposes, it created a nightmare for drug enforcement officials. What are the legal implications of medicinal marijuana use? What are the medical alternatives? Most materials on this topic have been published since 1997.

- ⋏ Is marijuana an effective remedy against pain? If so, is it fair to withhold it from patients?

- ⋏ What are the side effects of long-term marijuana use?

- ⋏ What are the legal ramifications; for example, state law versus federal law?

- ⋏ Will prescription marijuana undermine drug enforcement? How can it be controlled?

Background and Statistics

Addiction: Opposing Viewpoints

CQ Researcher (online version, *CQ Library,* also available)

National Survey of State Laws

Issues & Controversies on File (online version, *Facts.com,* also available)

Substance Abuse Sourcebook

The Library Catalog

Marijuana—law and legislation; Substance abuse; Hallucinogenic Drugs

Magazines and Newspapers

Newspapers and general magazines report on this topic. It lends itself to medical research and is an emotional topic. Try to find accurate medical information to support your viewpoint. For medical research, try a medical or health database such as the following:

HEALTH SOURCE PLUS—*Marijuana—therapeutic use; marijuana and medical*

MEDLINE—igm.nlm.nih.gov. This is a good source.

PAPER CHASE. This is a collection of several specific medical databases, including MEDLINE.

Your local newspaper or any newspaper. Online at www.ecola.com. (ecola is a Web site that links to online newspapers from all over the world. It's useful if you don't know the URL or the name of the newspaper in a particular locale.)

Internet

www.lindesmith.org/medicalmarijuana. Provides links to many essays and documents. Be sure to access the Fact Sheets and Quick Facts.

About.com's—law.about.com/newsissues/law/msub43.htm (for information on medicinal marijuana)

Megalaw—www.megalaw.com (to locate laws and cases by state; also includes federal law)

Cornell Law School—www.law.cornell.edu (for state statutes by broad topic or by state)

Agencies to Contact

American Council for Drug Education, 204 Monroe St., Suite 110, Rockville, MD 20850, 800-488-DRUG, www.acde.org/

National Clearinghouse for Drug Information, PO Box 2345, Rockville, MD 20852, 800-729-6686, www.health.org/aboutn.htm

Related Jumpstarts

See FDA and Medicine Approval

64 ➡ MERGERS AND MEGACOMPANIES

Search Terms

Corporate Reorganizations

Corporate Restructuring

Early Retirement Package

Layoffs and Payoffs

Mergers

Food for Thought

⌐ What has occurred to make mergers so widespread? Is this good? Bad? What are some of the repercussions?

⌐ What are the true benefits of merging and creating megacompanies? Is this trend safe for the economy?

⌐ Downsizing is a big part of merging. Is this contributing to unemployment? Who is affected by downsizing? (Downsizing may be treated as a separate topic.)

⌐ Does this trend affect feelings of company loyalty and the work ethic?

Background and Statistics

Congressional Quarterly Almanac

Issues & Controversies on File (online version, *Facts.com,* also available)

There are many books on specific companies that you might use. Financial records are available in books from Standard and Poors or Moody's (both available online).

The Library Catalog

Corporations—Acquisitions and Mergers; Downsizing of Organizations; Corporate Reorganizations; Organizational Change; Job Security; Layoff Systems

Magazines and Newspapers

Although there are many general articles, you may want to write about a large company that has recently merged. Be sure you search all databases and the Internet by that company name. Be specific by adding *merger* to your search. Any general, newspaper, or business database will be helpful, including the following:

ABI INFORM

ELECTRIC LIBRARY

PERIODICAL ABSTRACTS

Internet

Merger Enforcement Guidelines—strategis.ic.gc.ca/SSG/ct01280e.html. Contains good definitions and guidelines.

Thomas (Government Legislation Online)—thomas.loc.gov. Do a keyword search for government bills that deal with mergers and antitrust legislation.

Society for Human Resource Management—www.shrm.org

Agencies to Contact

To find information on preventing and coping with layoffs, contact:

Society for Human Resource Management, 1800 Duke St., Alexandria, VA 22314, shrm@shrm.org

Related Jumpstarts

See Changing Job Market; Superstores

65 NAFTA

Search Terms

North American Free Trade Agreement or NAFTA

FTAA (Free Trade of the Americas)

Fast Track

Texas (or another state) and Mexico and NAFTA

International Trade

Food for Thought

The North American Free Trade Agreement allows easier trade among member nations. Without tariffs, are U.S. companies moving their production to Mexico, where they can pay lower wages and lower their environmental costs? At this time, only the United States, Canada, and Mexico are part of NAFTA. You might consider finding statistics about success or failure and choose a side using historical data to support your position.

- Does the agreement affect survival of companies or employment in the United States?

- In what ways does this agreement affect the environment?

- Is it easier to smuggle drugs across the border? What other problems might occur?

- Is there a way to create fair taxing for U.S. highway use without discouraging foreign trade?

- Now that the agreement has been enforced for several years, has the economy benefited in expected ways?

- Should NAFTA be expanded to include all of the Americas?

Background and Statistics

CQ Researcher (online version, *CQ Library,* also available)—*North American Free Trade Agreement*

America's International Trade

Issues & Controversies on File (online version, *Facts.com,* also available)

West's Encyclopedia of American Law

The Library Catalog

Free Trade—North America; Trade—Mexico (etc.)

Magazines and Newspapers

If you live along the proposed NAFTA highway (I-69), this will be of interest and may be reported in your local newspaper. Use any business, general, or newspaper index, including

ABI INFORM

EBSCO HOST

PERIODICAL ABSTRACTS

WASHINGTON POST—www.washingtonpost.com

Internet

NAFTA Subject Guide—www.nhmccd.edu/lrc/kc/hot-topics.html. This site was created by librarians at Kingwood College and has many links for researchers.

The NAFTA Agreement—www.nafta.net/naftagre.htm (includes trade links)

Tracking U.S. Trade—lanic.utexas.edu/cswht/tradeindex

NAFTA secretariat—www.nafta-sec-alena.org

Hint: Look up your state highway department.

Agencies to Contact

Economic Policy Institute, 1660 L St. NW, Suite 1200, Washington, DC 20036, 202-775-8810, www.epinet.org

Related Jumpstarts

See Illegal Immigration

66 → NON-TRADITIONAL FAMILY

Search Terms

Family Values

Alternative (or Blended or Extended) Families

(Morality or Ethics) and Family

Family and Society and Changes

Religion and Family

Food for Thought

Non-traditional families as a topic can cover anything from changing values to types of new families, including extended, blended, alternative, single-parent, gay, or adoptive. If you like the idea but do not know how to proceed, we suggest you read a little from the first two or three books in the "Background and Statistics" list for ideas on refining this to a manageable topic. Select an issue such as "Fathers as head of single-parent families." We even found a lot of information on "grandparents raising grandchildren." Be sure to narrow the topic, or you will be frustrated by too much information that does not fit together.

Background and Statistics

Consider searching sources for earlier years to compare how people felt about an issue 10 or more years ago. After you select your topic, you will be able to find other reference sources that will be helpful. This is an area where statistics can help you prove your case.

American Attitudes

CQ Researcher (online version, *CQ Library,* also available)—*Families*

Facts on File

Growing Up in the 20th Century America

Into the Third Century [Information Plus Series]

The Gallup Poll. This is a good resource for comparing changing public opinion.

The Library Catalog

Family life; Family relations; Family values

Magazines and Newspapers

Books may be the best source for this topic, although much academic research has been done on the family and is reported in journals. Any general database will be helpful. Use alternative keywords to find useful articles about your specific topic.

HUMANITIES FULLTEXT INDEX. Covers research from principally academic sources.

PERIODICAL ABSTRACTS—*Family and society and change*

Internet

Use a government search engine to find agencies that have information on your topic. Search by keyword; for example, *changing family values.*

Government Printing Office—www.access.gpo.gov/su_docs

North Harris College—nhclibrary.nhmccd.edu/govinfo/us/search.html. A collection of government search engines.

Health and Human Services—www.hhs.gov

Also try

Family Pride Coalition—Gay and Lesbian Parents — www.familypride.org

Related Jumpstarts

See Divorce—No-Fault; Dual Career Families; Same-Sex Marriage

67 OZONE LAYER

Search Terms

Atmospheric Ozone

Montreal Protocol

Ozone or Ozone Layer

Greenhouse Effect

Food for Thought

Modern technology is blamed for damage to the ozone layer miles above the Earth. Developed nations have agreed in the Montreal Protocol to stop producing some offending products, but they have not convinced developing nations to do the same. There is a great deal of controversy among scientists about the level of harm that has been done. If you select this topic, do your homework. Get good background information—the newer the information, the better.

⅄ What has caused the environmental problems we have today? Is there proof?

⅄ What can be done to repair the damage?

⅄ Does it directly affect us now? What about future generations?

⅄ What is the government's role in this issue?

⅄ What laws have been passed by Congress to clean up the air and the environment? (Use them in your research.)

Consider researching a single aspect of this enormous problem; for example, whether the greenhouse effect is the cause of the warming weather conditions.

Background and Statistics

CQ Researcher (online version, *CQ Library,* also available)—*Ozone* or *Environment*

Encyclopedia of Climate and Weather—Ozone Hole

Gale Encyclopedia of Science—Ozone Layer Depletion

Pollution: Opposing Viewpoints

Weather Almanac—Ozone Layer Depletion

The Library Catalog

Ozone Layer Depletion; Atmospheric Ozone; Air—Pollution; Greenhouse Effect; Global Warming

Magazines and Newspapers

Look for scientific articles on this topic. There are plenty of journals that a layperson can understand. Don't forget about locating a law or two. The best resources are articles in a health or general index, such as the following:

HEALTH SOURCE PLUS—*Ozone Layer Depletion* (for an index to medical articles)

PERIODICAL ABSTRACTS—*Montreal Protocol; ozone and environmental protection*

WESTLAW. If you have access to this database, look up specific environmental laws.

PAPERCHASE. Includes MEDLINE and various other specific medical databases.

Internet

Ohio State Subject Guide—www.cis.ohio-state.edu/hypertext/faq/usenet/ozone-depletion/top.html

Environment Assignment Guide—www.nhmccd.edu/lrc/kc/environment-Internet .html

Environmental Protection Agency (EPA)—www.epa.gov/

Ozone Depletion Laws, Regulations, and Facts—www.epa.go/docs/ozone

U.S. Department of Energy Ozone Depletion Web Page—www.epa.gov/docs /ozone/index.html

Library of Congress—thomas.loc.gov. Search this government site by word or phrase for bills relating to clean air and the environment. The *Congressional Record* is especially useful.

Megalaw—www.megalaw.com (to locate laws and cases by state; also includes federal law)

Cornell Law School—www.law.cornell.edu (for state statutes by broad topic or by state)

Agencies to Contact

Committee for the National Interest for the Environment, 1725 K St., NW, Suite 212, Washington, DC 20006, 202-520-5810, cnie@cnie.org www.cnie.org/nle /air-3.html

Related Jumpstarts

See Greenhouse Effect

68 → POLICE BRUTALITY

Search Terms

Police and (Brutality or Misconduct or Abuse or Excessive Force)

Police and (Corruption or Complaints or Reform)

Police Misconduct

Police Conduct

Police and Ethical Behavior

Food for Thought

Believe it or not, there have always been rumors charging police misconduct. This is a topic you may want to argue either side of and for which there will be plenty of information, especially in newspapers. It is a high-profile topic, so if you choose it, try to keep your line of reasoning professional and use valid sources to reinforce your argument. Following are a few questions to get you focused:

⅄ What constitutes excessive force?

⅄ What role do race or other prejudices play in police violence? Research the Rodney King case and other more recent court cases.

⅄ What are possible solutions for preventing police misconduct?

⅄ Is punishment for police who have been convicted always fair and consistent?

⅄ Would the use of civilian review boards be more effective?

⅄ What about police rights?

⅄ Is violence an integral part of police work? Could it be a reaction to the work environment, or an attribute of the people attracted to the profession?

⅄ Is general ethical behavior a part of this problem?

Background and Statistics

CQ Researcher (online version, *CQ Library*, also available)

Encyclopedia of Crime and Justice—Police Misconduct

Police Brutality: Opposing Viewpoints.

Police Brutality: A National Debate

The Library Catalog

Police Malpractice; Police Complaints; Police Corruption; Police Brutality; Police Conduct

Magazines and Newspapers

Use any general magazine or newspaper index. Look up general terms and also specific cases.

ELECTRIC LIBRARY (for transcripts of national broadcasts on CNN, NPR, ABC, and others)

Online newspapers—www.ecola.com

PERIODICAL ABSTRACTS

Internet

The Internet has quite a few good locations for this topic, and *police brutality* works fairly well as a search phrase. You may spend your time more wisely by looking at books and journal databases. About.com has a nice collection of articles about police brutality, on both sides. Use the search engine to locate them.

Police Misconduct Complaint Center—www.policeabuse.com/

ACLU—Police Abuse—www.aclu.org/library/fighting_police_abuse.html

Megalaw—www.megalaw.com (to locate laws and cases by state; also includes federal law)

Cornell Law School—www.law.cornell.edu (for state statutes by broad topic or by state)

The Role of Penalty Schedules in Managing Police Misconduct—www.memphiscrime .org/research/whitepapers/wp5.html (a White Paper)

Agencies to Contact

American Civil Liberties Union (ACLU), 122 Maryland Ave. NE, Washington, DC 20002, 202-544-1681, aclu.org/

The Police Complaint Center, 4244-223 W. Tennessee St., Tallahassee, FL 32304, netrunner.net/pcc/index.htm

Related Jumpstarts

See Human Rights of Prisoners; Youth Crime

69 → POLITICAL CORRECTNESS

Search Terms

Political? Correct?

Political Correctness

Multiculturalism

Politically Correct

Gender Words

Food for Thought

We think of the phrase "political correctness" as an invention of the 1990s. Actually, the term "politically correct" was first mentioned in a Supreme Court case in 1793. In the 1930s, the phrase was used by the Stalinists in the Soviet Union. The negative connotations of this term are fairly recent. For a more positive point of view, use the word "multiculturalism." On this topic, you could simply be talking about using gender words correctly; for example, chairperson instead of chairman. How important is political correctness in today's society? Have we taken concerns about gender bias too far? Not far enough? Are we taking our correctness to ridiculous extremes? You might have fun with this topic. There are a few standup comedians who love this topic.

Background and Statistics

CQ Researcher (online version, *CQ Library,* also available)

Culture Wars: Opposing Viewpoints

Issues & Controversies on File (online version, *Facts.com,* also available)

Multiculturalism in Academe

The Library Catalog

Political Correctness; multiculturalism

Look specifically for *Illiberal Education,* an excellent book that discusses this topic.

Magazines and Newspapers

Use any newspaper, general, or business index, including

ABI—*Political Correctness; multiculturalism*

Newspapers online—www.ecola.com. This site will take you to a list of online newspapers. Use *Politically Correct* to search.

PERIODICAL ABSTRACTS—*Political Correctness; multiculturalism*

Internet

Use *Political Correctness* as a keyword or try the following addresses for fun and perhaps a quotation:

Politically correct cartoons—www.huberspace.com/cartoons/

From Political Correctness to Constitutional Law—www.wcl.american.edu/pub/faculty/boyle/identity.htm

The Pitfalls of Political Correctness—www.blind.net/bpg00005.htm. This is a very good article about the dangers of pretentious euphemisms.

Center for the Study of Popular Culture—www.cspc.org. This site focuses on "Political correctness, multiculturalism and other follies." This organization publishes articles and engages in legal activism.

Related Jumpstarts

See Work Ethic; Gender Differences

70 → RAPE

Search Terms

Rape or Date Rape or Acquaintance Rape

Sexual Assault

Sex Crimes

Use the terms listed in "Food for Thought" for specific crimes

Food for Thought

This topic is extremely broad and as old as time. Date rape and male rape are newer facets of this topic. Pick a single argument that interests you and refine it. Consider the psychological damage to rape victims. See if you can find information about what causes men (or women) to commit rape.

- Acquaintance or Date Rape
- Spousal Rape; Statutory Rape; Male Rape; Incest
- Victim's psychological trauma
- Should rape victims file charges? Is it worth the mental anguish?
- Do the courts mete out appropriate punishment for this crime?

Background and Statistics

CQ Researcher (online version, CQ Library, also available)

Encyclopedia of Crime and Justice

Encyclopedia of Marriage and the Family

Rape in America, A Reference Handbook

Statistical Handbook on Violence in America

The Library Catalog

Rape; Rape Victims; Acquaintance Rape; Sexual Harassment of Women; Women—Crimes Against

Magazines and Newspapers

Virtually all indexes and databases will contain articles on this topic. Think about the focus your research is taking and select the database accordingly; that is, if your focus is psychological or medical, use a medical database:

ELECTRIC LIBRARY—*Rape*

HEALTH SOURCE PLUS—*Acquaintance rape; Rape victims; Statutory rape; Rape; Male rape; Rape trauma syndrome*

MEDLINE *Rape*—igm.nlm.nih.gov. This is a good source for information on victims' trauma.

PERIODICAL ABSTRACTS—*Rape; (date or acquaintance) rape; Statutory rape; males and rape*

Internet

Please search carefully, using .org or .edu online domains because the terms you use can bring up pornography. There are many rape center hotlines online. Try to find them. You might include the word *counseling* in your search.

Sexual assault information page—www.cs.utk.edu/~bartley/saInfoPage.html

Megalaw—www.megalaw.com (to locate laws and cases by state; also includes federal law)

Cornell Law School—www.law.cornell.edu (for state statutes by broad topic or by state)

Men Working to End Men's Violence Against Women—www.whiteribbon.ca/students .htm. This site contains an education and action kit.

Wider Opportunities for Women Online—www.wowonline.org

Agencies to Contact

RAINN, Rape, Abuse and Incest National Network, 252 Tenth St. NE, Washington, DC 20002, Hotline—512-476-1866, www.rainn.org

Rape crisis centers have special counseling sessions for rape victims and parents. Your city probably has one. Check your local telephone book.

Related Jumpstarts

See Sex Offender Notification; Sexual Harassment in the Workplace

71 → RECYCLING

Search Terms

Recycling and (Plastic, Aluminum, Paper)

Reuse

Waste Reduction

Medical Waste and Ethics

Food for Thought

The younger generation has been very interested in finding ways to protect their environment. One thing we can all do is to recycle. This becomes a problem in areas where there is no pickup or ready source for receiving recycled articles. Think about the following questions:

- Is there a market for recycled materials?

- Is it cost-effective? Is recycling so important that cost-effectiveness should not be an issue?

- What is the cost to the city or county for recycling pickup and delivery? Is it economical? If not, should recycling be a moral issue?

- Is recycling by city waste companies done in primarily upper class neighborhoods? Is this arguable? (Do your homework by phone!)

- Consider the market for these products: plastic, aluminum, paper, and medical waste

Background and Statistics

CQ Researcher (online version, *CQ Library,* also available)

Issues & Controversies on File—Recycling

Pollution: Opposing Viewpoints

Recycling in America

Statistical Record of the Environment

Texas Environmental Almanac (Other states have the equivalent of this book.)

The Library Catalog

Recycling (Waste) Aluminum Recycling; Paper Recycling; Plastic Recycling

Magazines and Newspapers

Try a business or medical database for this topic. Watch out for too much information.

ABI INFORM—*Recycling and material or "advantages"* (for the business side of recycling)

ELECTRIC LIBRARY—*Recycling.*

CINAHL—*Recycling* (for medical waste)

Online newspapers at www.ecola.com

PERIODICAL ABSTRACTS

Internet

Recycler's World—www.recycle.net/recycle/index.htm—Descriptions and markets for recyclables

Marketplace for Industry Professionals—SolidWaste.com

Environment Subject Guide—www.nhmccd.edu/lrc/kc/environment-Internet.html

Consumer Recycling Guide—www.obviously.com/recycle

Agencies to Contact

Each city will have a recycling program. If you don't find it online or in the telephone book, call the local waste pickup services.

Related Jumpstarts

See Greenhouse Effect; Ozone Layer

72 ➤ ROAD RAGE

Search Terms

Road Rage

Driving and Anger

Aggression and Driving or Aggressive Driving

Aggression/Aggressiveness

Driving Stress

Food for Thought

In *Riding the Iron Rooster*, Paul Theroux states that the reason Texans are such courteous drivers is because each thinks the other has a gun in the front seat. That may not be 100 percent true, but it is true that drivers are not always courteous on busy freeways. Perfectly nice people turn into power-obsessed demons when they get behind the wheel of a vehicle. And each year the problem increases. The phenomenon called "road rage" is escalating in major cities around the country. Aggressive driving was involved in two-thirds of auto deaths in 1996. Use the Internet or books to locate the Insurance Institute highway statistics for accurate and current information on this topic. The librarian will help you find psychological causes for this trend.

⅄ What are the causes of road rage? What can be done to prevent it?

⅄ What solutions are being attempted to solve this serious problem?

⅄ Is road rage happening primarily in overpopulated cities? If so, what are the causes? The effects? The possible solutions?

Background and Statistics

CQ Researcher (online version, *CQ Library*, also available)—*Aggressive Driving*

Encyclopedia of Psychology—Aggression

Road Rage: Causes and Dangers of Aggressive Driving

Road Rage: Aggressive Driving

Each state publishes road statistics annually. Write or call your state highway patrol or department of transportation for yours.

The Library Catalog

Automobiles—Social Aspects; Anger; Aggressiveness; Road Rage

Magazines and Newspapers

Driving stress and *road rage* are the most appropriate terms for this topic. Use general indexes to find articles:

HEALTH SOURCE PLUS. Use *driving stress* here for best results (psychology journals).

Online newspapers at www.ecola.com

PERIODICAL ABSTRACTS—*(Automobile Driving or Traffic Accidents) and (Aggressiveness or Anger)*

Internet

Road Rage—www.aloha.net/~dyc/index.html

Aggressive Driving Organization—www.aggressivedriving.org

CNN Road Rage—www.cnn.com/US/9707/18/aggressive.driving

Browse all of Yahoo's links, which include articles, surveys, quizzes, and a brochure on how to avoid road rage from the American Automobile Association. Search.yahoo.com/bin/search?p=road+rage.

Agencies to Contact

AAA Foundation for Traffic Safety, 1440 New York Ave. NW, Suite 201, Washington, DC 20005, 202-638-5944, aainfo@aaafts.org, www.aafts.org

Related Jumpstarts

See Criminal Psychology; Drunk Driving; Gun Control

SAME-SEX MARRIAGE

73

Search Terms

Same-sex Marriages
(Gay or Homosexual or Lesbian) and Marriage
Defense of Marriage Act or Anti-Marriage Bill
Commitment Ceremonies

Food for Thought

This topic comes and goes, but is part of our changing social views. As gay and lesbian groups become stronger, it will be interesting to see what happens with this topic.

- Should gays and lesbians have the legal right to marry their same-sex partners?

- Is this a moral, religious, or government issue? *Legislated morality* is a phrase used with this topic.

- Because they cannot marry, homosexuals do not have access to certain government and other services. Should homosexuals be entitled to spousal benefits? Insurance? Tax benefits?

Background and Statistics

CQ Researcher (online version, *CQ Library*, also available)—*Same-sex marriage*

Encyclopedia of Homosexuality—*Marriage*

Homosexuality: Opposing Viewpoints

Issues & Controversies on File (online version, *Facts.com*, also available)—*Homosexuality and Same-sex marriage debate*

National Survey of State Laws

The Rights of Lesbians and Gay Men

Same Sex Marriage: Pro and Con: A Reader

The Library Catalog

Homosexuality—Law and Legislation, Gay Rights, Gay Couples, Same-Sex Marriage

Magazines and Newspapers

The newspapers and journals will be your safest and best sources of information on this topic. Any general index will help, and newspapers, particularly those from the state you may be researching, will have plenty of information. Do not forget to search state and local law. Any newspaper or general index will cover this topic, including the following:

ACADEMIC INDEX

ELECTRIC LIBRARY. This is a collection of transcripts from news shows; look at the current issues section listed under *Gay rights.* There are several transcripts from networks such as NPR, CNN, and PBS, all of which are highly reputable.

Online newspapers at www.ecola.com. Check articles from online big city papers such as *The New York Times, The Los Angeles Times,* or *The Miami Herald.* These cities have large homosexual populations.

PERIODICAL ABSTRACTS

Internet

This is definitely an area where you will encounter pornography. Be cautious. Remember, the domains .org, .gov, and .edu are generally more research oriented and definitely safer where pornography is concerned. *Same-sex marriage* is the best way to search this topic. For more specific information, try a state and your search terms; for example, *Montana and same-sex marriage.*

Thomas—thomas.loc.gov. Search the Defense of Marriage Act or Anti-Marriage Bill.

Megalaw—www.megalaw.com (to locate laws and cases by state; also includes federal law)

Cornell Law School—www.law.cornell.edu (for state statutes by broad topic or by state)

Mining Co. Search Engine Collection—marriage.miningco.com/msubgay.htm

Freedom to Marry Organization—www.ftm.org

League of Gay and Lesbian Voters—www.lglv.org

Religious Tolerance Organization—www.religioustolerance.org/hom_marr.htm. All sides of the issue are presented by this group.

Agencies to Contact

Freedom to Marry Coalition, 120 Wall St., Suite 1500, New York, NY 10005, 212-809-8585 X205, lldef@ftm.org www.ftm.org

Related Jumpstarts

See Non-traditional Family

74 ➔ SCHOOL CHOICE AND VOUCHERS

Search Terms

Educational Vouchers or School Aid to Education

Charter Schools

School Finance Reform

School Choice or School Vouchers

Equality of Education

Privatization of Schools

Edgewood v. *Kirby*

Food for Thought

The book *Public Schooling in America* has a very good rudimentary entry on equality of educational opportunity. You may want to start by reading the pertinent chapter. In school voucher programs, state and local government give parents monetary vouchers that they can use at any public or private school, allowing for choice in each student's education.

⌃ Are vouchers a plausible way to ensure that U.S. children receive the same quality of education?

⌃ What are charter schools? Will charter schools work?

⌃ What are the benefits or detriments of offering vouchers to U.S. families?

⌃ How can these school choices work and be fair to rich and poor alike?

⌃ What affect would voucher programs have on the inner city student?

Background and Statistics

CQ Researcher (online version, *CQ Library*, also available)—*Elementary and Secondary Schools; School Choice*

Education [Information Plus Series]

Education: Opposing Viewpoints

Encyclopedia of Educational Research

Encyclopedia of Education

Issues & Controversies on File (online version, *Facts.com*, also available)—*Education*

The Library Catalog

Educational Vouchers; School Choice; Education—Finance; Education—Public Schools; State Aid to Education.

Magazines and Newspapers

Check an educational index first. Newspapers are good for reporting local opinion.

EDUCATION INDEX

ERIC—ericir.syr.edu/Eric. The studies and articles that it refers you to are written by experts on education.

Newspapers online at www.usanewspapers.com or www.ecola.com/news/press

PERIODICAL ABSTRACTS—*Vouchers and education*

WESTLAW (for *Edgewood* v. *Kirby* in Texas and other cases)

Internet

Education Reform Guide—www.nhmccd.edu/lrc/kc/ed-reform.html. This is a collection of links on the topic.

Thomas—thomas.loc.gov. Search online legislature nationally.

Megalaw—www.megalaw.com (to locate laws and cases by state; also includes federal law)

Cornell Law School—www.law.cornell.edu (for state statutes by broad topic or by state)

Center for Education Reform—www.edreform.com/ (Charter School Research)

Related Jumpstarts

See Year-Round Schools

75 → SCHOOL PRAYER

Search Terms

Prayer in the Public Schools

School Prayer

Religion and Public Schools

Freedom of Religion

Food for Thought

Most people have strong feelings about this controversial issue. If you choose it, be very professional in your presentation of facts. You might make your paper more interesting if you find useful information on the history of attitudes toward school prayer. We love to compare changes in public attitudes during a given period. Another very good comparison here would be belief about this issue in small towns versus large urban areas. Some of the issues to consider are:

- ⅄ Should school prayer be allowed, and if so, in what form (silent meditation, actual prayers said aloud)?

- ⅄ Should graduation ceremonies, sports events, and other public school gatherings have invocations?

- ⅄ What responsibility do we have to people of differing faiths in a multicultural society?

- ⅄ How can we incorporate prayer and observe other religions?

- ⅄ Should state or national government be allowed to legislate this issue?

Background and Statistics

CQ Researcher (online version, *CQ Library,* also available)—*Elementary and Secondary Schools*

Issues & Controversies on File (online version, *Facts.com,* also available)—*School Prayer*

School Prayer: The Court, the Congress, and the First Amendment

Be sure to check the library's holdings for the books and articles listed in the bibliographies in these sources.

The Library Catalog

Prayer in the Public Schools; Religion in the Public Schools; Church and Education; Freedom of Religion

Magazines and Newspapers

The December 2000 issue of *Texas Monthly* magazine contains a great section on school prayer. It is worth finding. For articles, use any education, general, or newspaper index, including the following:

ELECTRIC LIBRARY. This database provides full-text transcripts of television and radio programs on the major networks.

EDUCATION INDEX (for educational articles)

ERIC—ericir.syr.edu/Eric—includes educational research and articles.

PERIODICAL ABSTRACTS

Internet

Links to both sides of this issue—ccwf.cc.utexas.edu/~ckramer

American Civil Liberties Union—www.aclu.org/library/aaprayer.html

Anti-Defamation League—www.adl.org/religion_ps/background.html

Megalaw—www.megalaw.com (to locate laws and cases by state; also includes federal law)

Cornell Law School—www.law.cornell.edu (for state statutes by broad topic or by state)

Agencies to Contact

Organization fighting for prayer in schools: Natural Prayer Project, 800-209-9929, naturlprayer@earthlink.net

Organization fighting to keep prayer out of schools: National Office of the Freedom from Religion Foundation, PO Box 750, Madison, WI 53701, www.ffrf.org

Related Jumpstarts

See Honor System in Colleges

SCHOOL VIOLENCE

76

Search Terms

Juvenile Homicide

School Safety

School Violence

Violence (in ERIC and MEDLINE)

Food for Thought

Sometimes we think public schools are becoming war zones. From urban schools to suburban, none of our schools seems safe for children. Gangs and other groups seem to proliferate. Each year the violence seems to originate from younger students. Is this a new phenomenon, or has it just been more widely publicized recently? What causes a student to become violent? What are reasons for the change? What can be done about it? Can schools teach nonviolence successfully? Should schools provide better preventive counseling?

Consider focusing on the responsibilities of parents and school officials. Discuss a balance of safety with personal freedoms, like freedom of the press or the right to bear arms. Use some of the recent incidents in your paper. Try to find psychological effects and causes.

Background and Statistics

CQ Researcher (online version, *CQ Library,* also available)—*Students, crimes against*

Digest of Educational Statistics

Education Sourcebook

Matter of Fact

School Violence

School Violence: A Reference Handbook

School Violence: The Reference Shelf

Violence: Opposing Viewpoints

The Library Catalog

School Violence; Juvenile Delinquency; Gangs

Magazines and Newspapers

Education, medical, and general periodical and newspaper databases are all helpful for this topic. You cannot miss. Just know where you are headed because there is so much information. Narrow or refine your topic. You will probably want to consider specific cases of violence as part of your search.

CINAHL

ERIC—www.ed.gov/databases/ERIC_Digests/index. Use *school violence* because these digests give background information written by experts.

HEALTH SOURCE PLUS—*School Violence*

WASHINGTON POST or your local newspaper

MEDLINE—igm.nlm.nih.org—*Violence and (School or Student)*

PERIODICAL ABSTRACTS—*School Violence*

Internet

Department of Education Search Engine—search.ed.gov

U.S. Department of Justice—www.ojp.usdoj.gov

Center for the Prevention of School Violence—www.ncsu.edu/cpsv

School Violence Statistics—Department of Education—nces.ed.gov

Keep Schools Safe Organization—www.keepschoolssafe.org This site provides useful information for students, parents, law enforcement officers, and school officials.

Agencies to Contact

Center for the Prevention of School Violence, 20 Enterprise St., Suite 2, Raleigh, NC 27607-7375, 1-800-299-6054

Related Jumpstarts

See Dress Codes; Gangs; Gun Control

77 → SEX AND VIOLENCE ON TV

Search Terms

Telecommunications Act 1996

V-Chip or Television Rating System

Censorship and First Amendment and Television

Television and (Violence or Sex)

Children and Television and (Impact or Effect)

Television and Parent? and Violence

Food for Thought

⌃ What has research indicated are the effects of television violence and sex on children? On adults?

⌃ Do the violence and sex shown on television reflect a decaying of American morals?

⌃ Should television have a more rigorous rating system? How successful are the blocking technologies, such as the V-chip?

⌃ Should television share the responsibility for violence and crime in our society?

⌃ What are parental responsibilities in supervising what children see on television?

⌃ What responsibility should the media have in selecting what they show on television?

⌃ Think about First Amendment rights.

Background and Statistics

CQ Researcher (online version, *CQ Library*, also available)—*Television—Violence*

Crime and Criminals: Opposing Viewpoints

The Gallup Poll includes statistics from public opinion surveys on how much people watch television and television's effect on children

Issues & Controversies on File (online version, *Facts.com*, also available)—*Television and Radio Content*

Mass Media: Opposing Viewpoints

Media Violence: Opposing Viewpoints

The Library Catalog

Violence in Television; Sex in Television; Television—Censorship

Magazines and Newspapers

These will probably be your best sources. Newspapers, particularly, discuss television sex and violence. Try your local paper for information. Use any general or newspaper index, including

ELECTRIC LIBRARY. This database contains transcripts from TV and radio news shows; use the guided search or advanced search to find information on the V-chip, Telecommunications Act, and television violence.

Online newspapers at www.ecola.com

PERIODICAL ABSTRACTS. Try several searches. Be specific because there are many articles on this topic.

Internet

Thomas—thomas.loc.gov. Use the keywords *sex violence television* to find legislation on this topic.

Telecommunications Act Text—www.technologylaw.com

Center for Online Addiction—www.netaddiction.com/television_violence.htm. Describes the impact of media violence on children.

University of Minnesota Institute of Child Development—www.cyfc.umn.edu/Documents/C/E/CE1002.html. Bibliography of children and violence.

Agencies to Contact

Motion Picture Association of America, 1600 Eye St. NW, Washington, DC 20006, www.mpaa.org/, 202-293-1966

Related Jumpstarts

See Media Influence on Public Opinion

78 → SEX EDUCATION

Search Terms

Sex Education

Sex Instruction

Sex Counseling

(Add Other Defining Terms to these)

Food for Thought

The argument about whether parents or the schools should teach sex education is an old one. Find early legislation and articles in the library. Can you find a trend of changing public attitudes on this topic? Are schools and parents more or less conservative today? How does the school decide what is appropriate for the sex education curriculum? Following are a few of the age-old considerations:

⅃ Does sex education increase sexual activity?

⅃ Does sex education actually decrease teenage pregnancy?

⅃ Does sex education affect the use of safe sex methods by the young?

⅃ At what age or grade should sex education begin?

⅃ Whose responsibility is it to teach children about sex and other life issues?

Background and Statistics

CQ Researcher (online version, *CQ Library,* also available)—*Sex Education; Elementary and Secondary Education*

Encyclopedia of Educational Research

Legal Rights of Women—Education

Statistical Handbook on Adolescents in America

Teenage Sexuality: Opposing Viewpoints

The Library Catalog

Sex Education; Sex Instruction

Magazines and Newspapers

Educational indexes like ACADEMIC and ERIC will be your best bet, because this topic is about school curriculum. Use education, health and medical, general, and newspaper indexes, including

ACADEMIC INDEX

CINAHL. This nursing and allied health database will be excellent for this search. Many psychology journals are included here.

ERIC—ericir.syr.edu/Eric. Covers educational research; a very good place to look for this information.

MEDLINE—igm.nlm.nih.org—*Sex Education* as a MeSH heading

Internet

Legislation relating to the provision of sex education in schools—www.avert.org /legislation.htm

Chicago Tribune article listing schools teaching sex education—cnews.tribune.com /news/tribune/story/0,1235,tribune-nation-78149,00.html

Megalaw—www.megalaw.com (to locate laws and cases by state; also includes federal law)

Cornell Law School—www.law.cornell.edu (for state statutes by broad topic or by state)

Be careful with this "tricky" Internet topic because of the pornography on the Web. Use the keywords *sex education in schools* for a promising, fairly safe search. You may elect to do an advanced search for sites with domains like .gov, .edu, or .org. The most pertinent research information will be found on free online databases, such as ERIC or MEDLINE (see above).

For maximum safety, use a good search engine (we like Yahoo) and try a domain search such as domain: edu and "sex instruction".

Agencies to Contact

Council for Sex Information and Education (CSIE), 2272 Colorado Blvd. #1228, Los Angeles, CA 90041

Sex Information and Education Council of the United States, 130 West 42nd St., Suite 350, New York, NY 10036, 212-819-9770, www.siecus.org, siecus@siecus.org

Related Jumpstarts

Rape; Sex Offender Notification

79 → SEX OFFENDER NOTIFICATION

Search Terms

Sex Offender Notification

Disclosure and Sex Crimes

Child Sexual Abuse and Prevention

Megan's Law

Judge John Bissell

Recidivism

Pedophiles (be cautious on the Internet)

Food for Thought

WARNING: This is a topic which, on the Internet, can turn up a lot of pornography. Be careful. We encourage you to use books, newspapers, and journal articles. This topic discusses whether a community should be notified when a convicted rapist, child molester, or other type of sex offender moves into the area. Statistics can be very helpful in defending your argument.

⌐ Is notification an infringement of the offender's civil rights?

⌐ What are the arguments for and against notification? Are there statistics available that would support pro or con arguments on this topic?

⌐ What has prompted some communities to press for notification? (Search for communities where this has happened and use one as a case study.)

Background and Statistics

Congressional Quarterly. Note the bibliography and list of agencies with addresses and telephone numbers

CQ Researcher (online version, *CQ Library,* also available)—*Crime and Criminals*

Issues & Controversies on File (online version, *Facts.com,* also available)—*Sex Offenders*

The Library Catalog

Sex crimes; Child sexual abuse—prevention

Magazines and Newspapers

Search the newspapers and journals for specific legislation or examples. Use any general or newspaper databases, including

NATIONAL NEWSPAPER INDEX or any online newspaper—www.ecola.com may be your best source

PERIODICAL ABSTRACTS

Internet

For maximum safety from pornography, use a good search engine and the advanced search engine (we like Google) or try a domain search such as domain:org and sex offender and notification.

Megan's Law—www.co.camden.naj.us/prosecutor/megans.htm

Sex offender registries by state—www.prevent-abuse-now.com/register.htm

Thomas—thomas.loc.gov. Use keyword searching to find current legislation.

Megalaw—www.megalaw.com (to locate laws and cases by state; also includes federal law)

Cornell Law School—www.law.cornell.edu (for state statutes by broad topic or by state)

Easton Massachusetts Police Department Notice—www.eastonpd.com/sexoff.htm

Teacher's Manual: Sex Education 7th grade—www.yale.edu/ynhti/curriculum/units/1981/3/81.03.09.x.html. Critique this manual.

Agencies to Contact

Pro-Notification Organization, National Center for Missing and Exploited Children, 2102 Wilson Blvd., Suite 550, Arlington, VA 22201-3052, 800-THE LOST or 703-235-3900, www.missingkids.org

Anti-Notification Organization, American Civil Liberties Union, 132 West 43rd St., New York, NY 10036, 212-944-9800, www.aclu.org

Related Jumpstarts

See Rape

80 ➤ SEXUAL HARASSMENT IN THE WORKPLACE

Search Terms

Sexual Harassment and (Workplace or Job or Employ?)

Women (or Men) and Workplace

Employment Discrimination and Legislation

Workplace Violence

Food for Thought

Sexual harassment is another topic about which there is almost too much information. Try to focus on a certain aspect of this topic and perhaps find legislation and specific examples. You may be wise to locate a case to research and comment on. Look at the law. It has changed, and there are specific guidelines on exactly what constitutes sexual harassment. You may want to include the guidelines in your paper. Keep in mind that this is a separate issue from violence against women. Sexual harassment does not have to be men harassing women. It may be more interesting to find some of the unusual cases.

Background and Statistics

CQ Researcher (online version, *CQ Library,* also available)—*Sexual Harassment.* One entry, "Crackdown on Sexual Harassment," is particularly good. These entries describe history and suggest future developments and contain a helpful bibliography.

Encyclopedia of Career Changes and the Work Forces

Feminism: Opposing Viewpoints

Issues & Controversies on File (online version, *Facts.com,* also available)—*Employment and Sexual Harassment*

The Legal Rights of Women (for legislation on this topic)

Working Women: Opposing Viewpoints

The Library Catalog

Sexual Harassment. There are excellent videos available on this topic. Watch for currency.

Magazines and Newspapers

Any business, general, or newspaper database is good for this topic. Look at the local newspaper for examples close to home.

ABI INFORM. Consider this the best source because its focus is business.

ELECTRIC LIBRARY. This database contains transcripts from television and radio programs.

NEWSPAPERS—www.ecola.com; your local newspaper

PERIODICAL ABSTRACTS. This is another good database if you use limiting keywords. Try *sexual harassment and (job or employ?)* or *workplace.*

Internet

Equal Employment Opportunity Commission—www.eeoc.gov/docs/currentissues .html

Thomas—thomas.loc.gov. Use a keyword search for the legislation on this topic.

Megalaw—www.megalaw.com (to locate laws and cases by state; also includes federal law)

Cornell Law School—www.law.cornell.edu (for state statutes by broad topic or by state)

Employer help topics—www.employerhelp.org

National Association of Women (NOW)—www.now.org

NOTE: This section focuses on the workplace, but you may want to consider sexual harassment in the military or an educational institution.

Agencies to Contact

See the list of Web sites above. EEOC and NOW are excellent sources for your questions. Prepare three or four questions and write or call the organizations. You may know a lawyer who has dealt with a sexual harassment case; if so, interview him or her.

Related Jumpstarts

See Gender Differences; Glass Ceiling

81 SINGLE-SEX SCHOOLS

Search Terms

Single Sex Schools

Single Sex Education

Sexism in Education

Sex Discrimination in Education

Separated by Sex

(Parochial or Church Schools) and Single Sex

Food for Thought

A recent study claims that boys are called on to answer questions more often and, in general, are given preferential treatment in the classroom. Why? What proof can you find of this favoritism? Other studies show that both girls and boys appear to learn more efficiently, have higher test scores, and gain more confidence without the opposite sex in the classroom. Why? If this is true, should Americans support public and private single-sex schools?

Background and Statistics

CQ Researcher (online version, *CQ Library,* also available)—*Elementary and Secondary Education.* Contains an excellent bibliography.

Issues & Controversies on File (online version, *Facts.com,* also available)—*Education*

The Library Catalog

Coeducation; Church Schools; Private Schools; Sex Discrimination in Education; Sexism in Education; Afro-American; Single-Sex Schools; Boys and Education; Girls and Education

Magazines and Newspapers

Search the education databases or any general database. You might want to look up specific cases in which women have enrolled in a formerly all-male school, like the Citadel, or the opposite has happened.

ACADEMIC INDEX—*Single and (sex or gender) and school*

EDUCATION INDEX

ERIC—www.ericir.syr.edu/Eric. Covers scholarly articles on education; many sources listed here will be published findings from studies and polls. Type in *Single Sex Schools.*

NEWSPAPERS ONLINE —www.ecola.com

Internet

The Internet is helpful, using *single sex schools,* but many Web sites listed may be advertisements for actual single-sex schools. Whenever you use sex for a search word, you will find there are many inappropriate articles. Make sure that what you find on the Web is suitable for your paper.

American Association of University Women—www.aauw.org

Bibliography of research documents on the topic—eric-web.tc.columbia.edu/alerts /ia73.html

Why an All-Girl School?—www.dsha.k12.wi.us/single4.htm

NOTE: Try to pick one argument and select search words accordingly; for example, *single-sex school and learning opportunities.* This is an excellent topic for a visit or telephone call with a counselor or administrator at a school for one sex. Always prepare three or four pertinent questions before you make a visit or call.

Related Jumpstarts

See Gender Differences

82 → SOCIAL SECURITY REFORM

Search Terms

Social Security

Generation X

Medicare

Reform and Social Security

Food for Thought

It seems as though Congress is always studying Social Security. Baby boomers and Generation Xers are beginning to worry about their retirement future and the Social Security system. Narrow wisely; this is a broad and timely topic. The following are issues you may find interesting:

⌃ Privatization of Social Security

⌃ Government money management versus investing funds in the stock market or other investment means

⌃ Should Social Security be paid according to need? Contribution?

⌃ Survivors' benefits for children

⌃ Social Security numbers as identification and privacy

⌃ What plan is Congress considering to restructure Social Security? (You may want to argue in favor of or against.)

Background and Statistics

CQ Researcher (online version, *CQ Library,* also available)—*Social Security*

Issues & Controversies on File (online version, *Facts.com,* also available). Use the bibliography for further reading.

Encyclopedia of Social Work Volume 3—Social Security

The Library Catalog

Social Security—United States; Medicare. Try to find the newer books on this topic.

Magazines and Newspapers

Government databases are especially good for this topic. Second best are newspapers.

PERIODICAL ABSTRACTS

SIRS GOVERNMENT REPORTER

WASHINGTON POST or any other newspaper. Newspapers have good overview articles—www.ecola.com

Internet

Social Security Reform Guide—www.nhmccd.cc.tx.us/lrc/kc/soc-security.html. Research the past and present of SS. This library guide is from Kingwood College.

Social Security Administration—www.ssa.gov. The government has done an excellent job on this site of presenting Social Security information for the novice.

What every kid should know about Social Security + Teaching Guides—www.ssa.gov /kids

North Harris College—nhclibrary.nhmccd.edu/govinfo/us/search.html. Check this annotated list of government search engines.

Agencies to Contact

Social Security Administration, 1-800-772-1213. Use the yellow pages for your local SSA office.

Related Jumpstarts

See Health Insurance Debate; Tax Reform

83 ⟶ SPORTS AND LIFELONG BENEFITS

Search Terms

Sports and Lifestyle Management

Sports Psychology

Sports and Child Development

Sportsmanship

Exercise—Teen Health

Food for Thought

This is a great topic and offers many refinements. Consider whether the money spent to offer physical education to school children meets its goal of instilling lifelong good health habits.

- ⅄ Do athletics teach qualities or habits that people need for living?

- ⅄ Are there long-term benefits for those who run, walk, swim, and so forth?

- ⅄ What are the psychological, social, or physical benefits of sports? Sportsmanship? Teamwork? Mental or physical well-being?

- ⅄ What about the benefit of sports for girls?

- ⅄ Certainly consider the lifetime benefits of exercise for your health.

Background and Statistics

American Manhood

CQ Researcher (online version, *CQ Library*, also available)

Lessons of the Locker Room

Social Significance of Sport

Sports in America

Sports in Society: Issues and Controversy

The Library Catalog

Masculinity (psychology); School Sports; Sportsmanship; Sports—Philosophy and Theory

Magazines and Newspapers

Use any education, medical, health, and general indexes, including

ERIC—www.nhmccd.edu/lrc/kc/eric.html—*Sports psychology; Athletics and well-being; Athletics and self-actualization* (for abstracts of articles relating to sports in schools)

MEDLINE—igm.nlm.nih.gov—*Sports PX; Exercise PX; (Sports or exercise) and (psychology or physiology)* (for a health, rather than sports, point of view)

PERIODICAL ABSTRACTS—*Sports and child development.* (for abstracts of articles in both scholarly and general periodicals)

Internet

This is a tricky topic to find, but there *is* information on the Internet. Be persistent. Carefully evaluate what you find.

National Institutes of Health—www.nih.gov

About.com—*Search the keyword Exercise*—parentingteens.about.com/parenting/parentingteens/cs/exercise/index.htm. Provides Teen Health Links to information about the advantages of exercise.

Department of Education—www.ed.gov. Search using the terms listed previously. We found a few good sites.

NOTE: This topic is worth researching. Try refining it to health aspects of athletes in middle age or sportsmanship and the workplace. Team sports could be a part of this—just don't forget your focus. You might call a school physical education instructor for an interview. Education departments may have statistics about physical education in schools.

Related Jumpstarts

See Athletes as Role Models; Fitness for Children; Women's Athletics

84 → SPORTS ARENAS

Search Terms

Stadium Economics

Sports Facilities

Sports Arenas

Stadium Financing

Sports Benefits

Food for Thought

⋏ Who should pay the substantial costs of building new sports arenas?

⋏ Is it fair to use tax dollars to build sports arenas when so few citizens actually attend or can afford to attend games?

⋏ Can sports arenas revitalize downtown areas?

⋏ What are methods cities could incorporate to help offset substantial building and maintenance costs?

⋏ Should sports teams own or lease sports arenas? Should players?

⋏ Research Roger Noll and Robert Baade, who are experts in this field.

⋏ Select a city that has built or is building a stadium and do some research on it (e.g., Houston, Nashville, Denver).

Background and Statistics

CQ Researcher (online version, *CQ Library,* also available)—*Sports Arenas*

Pay Dirt

The Library Catalog

Sports—Economic Aspects—United States; Sports Facilities

Magazines and Newspapers

Newspapers seem to be the best source for this topic. Select a city with an arena and follow the newspaper articles for the period of time before a vote was taken on whether the city would pay for the stadium. Dallas, Houston, Los Angeles, and Phoenix are good choices. Also try any general database:

ACADEMIC INDEX—*Sports facilities and finance*

ELECTRIC LIBRARY—*Sports Facilities* (for transcripts of television news stories)

Your local newspaper if a new arena is planned in your area—*Sports Arenas and financing; sports facilities and financing*

Internet

Institute for Local Self Reliance—www.ilsr.org. Look at the "sports" section. Watch for bias; you want to represent all sides of the issue.

This topic was very hot for a while. Now stadiums seem to be a "given." If you choose this topic, it will probably be because your city is building a stadium. Search your local paper.

Agencies to Contact

To reiterate, look locally. If your city is building a stadium, there will definitely be a sponsoring group. Also look for the opposition. Try to find both sides of the issue.

Related Jumpstarts

See Downtown: Can It Be Saved?

85 → STANDARDIZED TESTS

Search Terms

Personnel Testing

Credentialing

Competency Testing

Competency Based Education

Search Specific Tests, TASP, SAT, ACT, GRE

Food for Thought

There has been much controversy about the validity and fairness of standardized tests. Colleges universally look at test grades, such as SAT and ACT, as part of entrance requirements. If you are in high school, you may want to look at tests given in your area. Texas has the TAAS test that must be passed for high school graduation and New York has the Regents exam. Following are a few points to consider:

⋏ Are standardized tests fair to people of different races or cultures? Are they biased against minorities or minority groups?

⋏ Several tests to consider are the TASP, SAT, and ACT. In Texas, students must take the TASP test to enter college. Most colleges nationwide insist that students make a certain score on a standardized test as part of entrance to the college. Does this (or any other) test give an accurate picture of student capabilities? Find support for your argument.

⋏ Choose a special group of people, for example, teachers, nurses, special education students, college entrance students, or high school graduates. Should tests be given to certify these groups?

Background and Statistics

Encyclopedia of Educational Research—Competency Testing

Education [Information Plus Series]

Encyclopedia of Management—Personnel Testing

Mental Measurements Yearbook

There are reference books that publish education statistics annually. Ask the librarian.

The Library Catalog

Competency based educational tests; Competency based education; Educational Tests and Measurements; Ability—Testing

Magazines and Newspapers

An education database like ERIC or Academic Index will probably be best for statistics and educational research and evaluation. Any business, education, or general index will also have information, including

ABI INFORM—*Personnel selection; Competency tests.* This is an index to business journals.

ERIC—ericir.syr.edu/About—*Teacher competency testing; Minimum competency testing* (students); *test wiseness.* This is an index to educational journals and research. You may write to AskEric and ask for statistics and specific information that you are having problems locating.

PERIODICAL ABSTRACTS—*Competency tests* (use topic search)

SIRS GOVERNMENT REPORTER—*competency testing.* (for full-text articles published by the government)

Internet

Standards and Assessment as Part of Effective Education—www.interlog.com /~klima/ed/standards.html. Essays from a variety of organizations.

Department of Education—search.ed.gov. Use the search engine. Type in *standardized tests*, then limit the results list to *fairness.*

Standardized tests and assessment measures—www.heinemann.com/info/08894f10 .html

Educational Testing Service—www.ets.org

Fair Test Organization—www.fairtest.org

Agencies to Contact

National Occupational Competency Testing Institute, notci@notci.org, www.nocti.org

Do not forget to talk to local colleges and public school systems.

Related Jumpstarts

See Affirmative Action; Community College Standards; Gender Differences

86 → STATE LOTTERIES

Search Terms

Lotteries

State Lotteries

Compulsive Gambling

Gambling

Food for Thought

Statistics show that gambling has gained wider national acceptance. Families go to Las Vegas for vacations—a place where children were invisible 15 years ago. Now state lotteries are more and more popular as a way for the state to raise money. If you consider this topic, you might look at it from a "moral or ethical" stance or from a "where does the money go?" viewpoint. Following are some questions to ask:

⌐ Do the benefits of lotteries outweigh their harmful effects (if any) on society? Name proven effects.

⌐ Have lotteries been responsible for changing our attitudes about the morality of gambling?

⌐ Are profits actually spent on earmarked programs, such as education? If so, does the state still give education its usual allocation so that it gains from the use of lottery money? Find examples.

⌐ What groups fight to end the lottery, and how and why do they do so?

⌐ Does the lottery actually bring promised money to the state? (There are states where the lottery has failed and states that have been successful; look for examples of each.)

Background and Statistics

Congressional Quarterly

CQ Researcher (online version, *CQ Library*, also available)—*Gambling*

Gambling [Information Plus Series]

Issues & Controversies on File (online version, *Facts.com*, also available)—*Lotteries*. Be sure to check the bibliography

The Library Catalog:

Lotteries; Gambling—Law; Gaming

Magazines and Newspapers

Use any newspaper or general databases, including

ELECTRIC LIBRARY. This provides transcripts from TV and radio news shows.

Any local newspaper is good for the local lottery; www.ecola.com has newspapers and journals you can search online.

PERIODICAL ABSTRACTS. This huge general index is a good starting point.

WESTLAW, a legal database, is great for looking up the legislation on lotteries. It is primarily available in academic or law libraries.

Internet

Megalaw—www.megalaw.com (to locate laws and cases by state; also includes federal law)

Cornell Law School—www.law.cornell.edu (for state statutes by broad topic or by state)

Gaming Industry Links—omni.cc.purdue.edu/~carlb/gambling.htm

Institute for Self Reliance—www.ilsr.org/newrules/sports.html. This is a great collection of information from costs to case studies. Definitely a slanted viewpoint. Look for both sides of the issue.

Ken White's Shazam—shazam.econ.ubc.ca/flip. Try a little first-hand research and record it for your paper.

Frontline Gambling Pro/Con—www.pbs.org/wgbh/pages/frontline/shows/gamble/procon

Agencies to Contact

National Coalition Against Legalized Gambling, 110 Maryland Ave. N.E, Washington, DC 20002, www.ncalg.org

North American Association of State and Provincial Lotteries, 1700 E. 13th St., Suite 4PE, Cleveland, OH 44114, 216-241-2310

State of Texas, General Lottery Information, 800-375-6886, 202-546-2254 (contact your state lottery agency)

Related Jumpstarts

See Gambling as a Moral Issue

SUICIDE IN ELDERLY

Search Terms

Use Suicide and (Age, Ethnic Group)

(Alternative Terms) Elderly—Aged—Older People—Old Age

Causes: Depression—Pain—Stress—Domestic Violence

Ethnic Groups—Blacks—Afro-Americans—Indians—Native Americans

Food for Thought

This is another interesting hot topic about which there is almost too much information. We know that both suicide and alcoholism are prevalent in the elderly. You will need to refine your topic; for example, "Suicide among the elderly who live alone" or "Alcoholism and suicide among the elderly." Select several keywords that help refine your subject. You might contact a nursing home or suicide hotline (main number only) and ask preselected questions. Consider many factors, including the following:

- What are the primary causes of suicide in the elderly? Find research and statistics.

- What kinds of intervention are successful in preventing repeated suicide attempts? Can treatment be successful in preventing suicidal behavior?

- What part does mental illness play in suicides? Loneliness? Depression?

- What success have national and local hotlines had in preventing suicides? Can you find statistics?

Background and Statistics

A Matter of Fact. Good for statistics and quotes.

Columbia University College of Physicians & Surgeons Complete Home Guide to Mental Health

Death and Dying: Opposing Viewpoints

Encyclopedia of Suicide

Healthy People 2000

Issues & Controversies on File (online version, *Facts.com,* also available)

Statistical Record of Health & Medicine

Suicide

Suicide: Opposing Viewpoint

The Library Catalog

Suicide; Suicide Prevention; Suicidal Behavior (as a keyword search); *Elderly* (and related words)

Magazines and Newspapers

Medical or health databases are good for research statistics and data. General databases have it all.

ELECTRIC LIBRARY (for transcripts of television news shows)

MEDLINE —igm.nlm.nih.gov

HEALTH SOURCE PLUS. This is an index to medical journals and pamphlets. There is some full text.

PERIODICAL ABSTRACTS

Internet

The Internet is particularly good for *elderly suicide.* Make sure the sites have reliable information.

American Association of Suicidology (AAS)—www.cyberpsych.org/aas.htm

Internet Mental Health—www.mentalhealth.com/p13.html. The site links users to a wealth of sites containing at least 10 pages of information on mental health, divided by subject.

National Administration on Aging—www.aoa.dhhs.gov/NAIC/Notes/suicide.html

Behavior Health Association—www.bha-inc.org/elderly_suicide_page.htm

Agencies to Contact

National health associations will have information. Find your local associations in the yellow pages. Also, think about homes for the elderly. Make a list of questions and call local retirement homes, nursing homes, or agencies.

Related Jumpstarts

See Assisted Suicide; Crimes Against the Elderly

88 SUPERSTORES

Search Terms

Wal-Mart (or another choice)

Superstore Sprawl

Small Business and Shopping Malls and Zoning

Competition and Superstore

Food for Thought

In the 1990s, we began to see more and more "superstores," or one-stop-shopping centers, for computers, food, clothing, hardware, books, automobiles, and now caskets. (Honestly; see www.budgetcasket.com.) How have these superstores affected the marketplace and the way we shop? Ask yourself the following questions:

- ⅄ In what ways have these stores affected small towns?
- ⅄ How have they affected "mom and pop" store owners?
- ⅄ Can small businesses compete with the buying power of these superstores?
- ⅄ Is indiscriminate expansion of superstores a national trend?
- ⅄ What will be the future of these stores?
- ⅄ Could there be a trend away from these huge stores?

Background and Statistics

CQ Researcher (online version, *CQ Library,* also available)

Facts on File—Department and Variety Stores

Moody's Handbook of Common Stocks. Select a company to research, such as K-Mart, Wal-Mart, or Barnes and Noble. Moody's gives current earnings and background information, recent development, and prospects for companies.

Value Line Investment Survey. This is similar to Moody's; look under *Retail Store Industry.*

Magazines and Newspapers

Newspapers and business journals should be your best sources of information for this topic. Try specific journals such as *Chain Store Age.*

ABI INFORM (for articles on small business and competition)

PERIODICAL ABSTRACTS (for information on Wal-Mart, discount department stores, and globalization)

Newspapers. Try your local paper.

Internet

Testimony to the Committee on the Judiciary for the National Alliance for Fair Competition—www.house.gov/judiciary/1041.htm

Federal Trade Commission—www.ftc.gov. Use the search engine. This is a very good choice.

American Bar Association—www.abanet.org/antitrust/committees/computer /win98meyers.html—Antitrust Law (computer)

Chain Store Age—www.chainstoreage.com/

Annoyed by Superstores—www.msbooks.com/msbooks/superstores.html (for articles arguing against superstores)

Agencies to Contact

National Alliance for Fair Competition, 3 Bethesda Metro Center, Suite 1100, Bethesda, MD 20814, 410-235-7116

International Mass Retail Association, 1901 Pennsylvania Ave., N.W., 10th Floor, Washington, DC 20006, 202-861-0774, www.imra.org

NOTE: If you live in a small town, this topic will definitely interest you. You might talk to local business people and find out the effects of a superstore on them. Call a few "mom and pops," then call the superstore manager. Consider contacting the Chamber of Commerce or other business groups.

Related Jumpstarts

See Mergers and Megacompanies; Downtown—Can It Be Saved?

89 → TAX REFORM

Search Terms

Tax? Reform and Plan

Flat-Rate Income Tax or Flat Tax

Tax Cut and Budget Deficit

Sales Tax

Food for Thought

Consider some of the following subtopics as ways of limiting this huge topic:

⋏ What are suggested methods of tax reform? Pick a method that interests you and locate both pro and con information about it.

⋏ Will a flat-rate income tax work? Who will be helped most by it? Would it be fair to all?

⋏ In a flat-rate tax system, would lack of tax breaks affect the incentive to risk owning a business?

⋏ Should we establish a national retail sales tax to replace the current income tax system?

⋏ Consider comparing the different political parties and their views on tax reform.

Background and Statistics

CQ Researcher (online version, *CQ Library,* also available)—*Taxation*

Issues & Controversies on File (online version, *Facts.com,* also available). Be sure to consult the bibliography at the end of each of these articles for more sources on this topic.

The Library Catalog

Flat-Rate Income Tax; U.S.—taxation; Income Tax; Tax Reform

Magazines and Newspapers

Newspaper and general indexes are best for this topic.

ELECTRIC LIBRARY. Contains transcripts of many television and radio specials on tax reform.

NATIONAL NEWSPAPER INDEX or any online newspapers at www.ecola.com

PERIODICAL ABSTRACTS

WASHINGTON POST INDEX—www.washingtonpost.com. Use the most recent two weeks.

Internet

Heritage Foundation—www.taxation.org—*Tax Reform Now*

Brookings Tax Reform—www.brook.edu/es/infocus/taxreform.htm. This is an interesting site. Be sure to look at both sides of the issue.

Americans for Tax Reform—www.atr.org

Agencies to Contact

Citizens for Tax Justice, 1311 L St. NW, Washington, DC 20036, 1-888-626-2622, www.ctj.org

Related Jumpstarts

See Health Insurance Debate; Social Security Reform; Welfare Reform

90 ➤ TERM LIMITS

Search Terms

Proposition 140

Term Limit? (Truncating allows for Limits and Limitations)

Term of Office

Congressional Term Limits

Food for Thought

Term limits have been considered since the days of the Articles of Confederation. Term limits place statutory limitations on the number of terms officeholders may serve. This has especially been discussed as a possibility for members of Congress. The issue of term limits became important in the United States during the late 1980s and early 1990s. Following are a few questions that might help you refine this topic:

- ↗ Would term limits eliminate the influence of lobbyists and special interest groups?

- ↗ Would they allow politicians to vote their conscience instead of worrying about the results of the next election?

- ↗ Or would term limits give politicians carte blanche to abuse their power, believing they will not be held accountable?

- ↗ Are we likely to get term limits when the people who would have to abide by them are the very ones who would write the legislation promoting them?

You might find good local or state examples of term limits. Whatever you do, be sure to find the viewpoints of both the proponents and the opponents.

Background and Statistics

Almanac of American Politics

CQ Researcher (online version, *CQ Library,* also available)—*Testing Term Limits*

Encyclopedia of the United States Congress

Issues & Controversies on File (online version, *Facts.com,* also available)—*Term Limits*

The Library Catalog

United States Congress—Term of Office; Term Limits

Magazines and Newspapers

Use any general or news index, including

ELECTRIC LIBRARY—*Term Limits*

NEWSPAPERS. Online newspapers, especially www.washingtonpost.com, will have articles of this timely topic. Try the Kingwood College collection of online newspapers at www.nhmccd.edu/lrc/kc/subjects.html#news.

PERIODICAL ABSTRACTS—*Term Limitations*

Internet

There is plenty of information on the Internet about term limits. Look at particular party platforms. Be careful that you get information from reliable sources. Several states have considered term limits. You may want to look by state and limit your paper to a single state and its results. Look at the pros and cons.

For progress on congressional bills, try *Thomas*—thomas.loc.gov/

Megalaw—www.megalaw.com (to locate laws and cases by state; also includes federal law)

Cornell Law School—www.law.cornell.edu (for state statutes by broad topic or by state)

US Term Limits—www.termlimits.org

Agencies to Contact

The League of Women Voters is an excellent source of information. Call, visit the online site, or write to your local or national agency:

League of Women Voters (National), 1730 M St., NW, Washington, DC 20036, 202-429-1965, www.lwv.org

Related Jumpstarts

See Ethics of Political Leaders

91 → TOBACCO REGULATIONS

Search Terms

Tobacco and Regulation

Smoking and Effects and (Teen?)

Nicotine or Cigarettes or Tobacco

Second Hand Smoke

Food for Thought

There is so much information on this topic that refining or narrowing will be crucial. Look for some of the original legislation. You will find some of the original research by tobacco companies online. Suggested subtopics include

- Government rights and responsibilities in prohibiting harmful behavior.
- Advertising—Is it aimed at teens?
- Smokeless tobacco—Better or worse?
- Liability of tobacco companies. Be sure to find the legislation.
- Smokers' rights versus non-smokers' rights.
- Second-hand smoke. Find the legislation.
- Do not forget to consider the health and insurance company issues.

Background and Statistics

Reducing the Health Consequences of Smoking: 25 Years of Progress

CQ Researcher (online version, *CQ Library,* also available)—*Tobacco*

Tobacco and Smoking: Opposing Viewpoints

Regulating Tobacco

The Library Catalog

Smoking; Tobacco; Tobacco Habit; Tobacco Law

Magazines and Newspapers

Use any health, business, government, news, or general index. Select according to the refined topic.

CINAHL (for tobacco-related illness). Use *tobacco in de* or *smoking in de* ("de" means descriptor or subject heading).

ERIC (for *smoking and schools*). Try the Subject Heading Lists, then limit.

MEDLINE (for tobacco-related illness)—igm.nlm.nih.gov. The Medical Subject Heading (MeSH) is *Tobacco Use Disorder.* You may have to have the library order the articles you locate, but it will be worth it.

Newspapers—www.ecola.com

PERIODICAL ABSTRACTS or any general index will have lots of information.

WESTLAW is especially good for this topic. The tobacco legislation is there. WESTLAW also has a section that includes small newspapers from around the country. Look at the newspapers of some of the tobacco-growing states and see what they have to say on the topic. Is their information slanted in a different way? These states will be concerned about jobs. If you don't have access to WESTLAW, use online newspapers.

Internet

Sunspot Health—sunspot.health.org/cgi-bin/ismoking.cgi

Bureau of Alcohol, Tobacco, Firearms—www.aft.treas.gov

Subject Guide from Wooster College—www.wooster.edu/Library/Gov/NewDocs /Tobacco.html

Thomas—thomas.loc.gov. Find government legislation by keyword.

Agencies to Contact

American Cancer Society, 6301 Richmond, Houston, TX 77057, 713-266-2877 www.cancer.org

You might also look up tobacco companies and write to them. An annual report would be interesting.

Related Jumpstarts

See Alcohol Advertising; FDA and Medicine Approval; Food Safety

92 → TORT REFORM

Search Terms

(Legal or Tort) Reform

Punitive Damages

Common Sense Product Liability Legal Reform Act

Food for Thought

If you are injured or suffer a loss as a result of another person's negligence, you are entitled to speedy, adequate compensation. If you do not receive that compensation, you have the right to present your case through a court of law by filing a "tort" lawsuit. But has this right gotten out of hand?

Slip on a wet floor at the mall and consider a lawsuit against the mall owner. Get cancer from smoking cigarettes and sue the tobacco companies. That is what many Americans do. It is our right. But is it right? Is our society becoming too litigious? If so, what are the causes? What are possible alternatives? Do lawsuits cost taxpayers and customers more money? How do they affect the costs of goods and services? What can or should be done to correct the current situation? Following are possible issues to discuss in your paper:

⅄ Should the law provide a set limit on particular torts to control punitive damages? For example, a slippery floor with no "Wet Floor" sign, $50,000 plus hospital expenses?

⅄ Would a legislative bill to limit damages be unfair to victims? Why? Why not?

⅄ You might argue generally about society and lawsuits. Be careful if you use this broad topic. Broad topics are generally hard to handle and confusing to the researcher and reader. State examples and find statistical and financial proof to use in your paper.

Background and Statistics

CQ Researcher (online version, *CQ Library,* also available)—*Torts*

State laws should be available at your public library, or look online at the sites listed under "Internet," below.

Magazines and Newspapers

Legal documents to back up your argument or viewpoint are available in some databases. Business, government, and general databases will work best for this topic, including

ELECTRIC LIBRARY (for transcripts from news shows)

WESTLAW. Search for cases, *product liability, tort law.* Sample search: *Punitive damages and (tort or legal? reform).* WESTLAW can be found in academic and law libraries.

Internet

Thomas—thomas.loc.gov

Megalaw—www.megalaw.com (to locate laws and cases by state; also includes federal law)

Cornell Law School—www.law.cornell.edu (for state statutes by broad topic or by state)

American Tort Reform Association—www.atra.org/atra/atra.hom. This bipartisan organization seeks fairness and balance in the U.S. legal system.

RAND Institute for Civil Justice—www.rand.org

Texans for Lawsuit Reform—www.tortreform.com/outside.html. Look up tort reform in your state. You should be able to find suits, then use the newspaper to find articles about them.

Most law schools have great collections of essays and articles on these topics. Find the law school online, then use its search engine to locate articles.

Related Jumpstarts

See Campaign Finance Reform

93 → WEB TV

Search Terms

Web TV

Enhanced TV

Interactive Television

Intercast

Food for Thought

Web TV gets you connected. Send e-mail to friends and family, surf the Internet, and interact with new forms of entertainment—all from your TV. Interactivity allows participants to play along with game shows, participate in polls, and chat with other viewers during programs. Questions to ask include the following:

Is Web TV the way we will all access the Web and each other?

Will easier access affect attempts to control the content?

Will companies be willing to build to accommodate this medium?

How will WebTV change family viewing?

Background and Statistics

Consumer Reports: "WebTV: The Internet Without a Computer."

Introducing WebTV

Complete Idiot's Guide to Surfing the Internet with WebTV

The Future of the Interactive Television Services Marketplace: What Should Consumers Expect? This government document is also available online at purl.access .gpo.gov/GPO/LPS10547

Check for new books on this new topic.

The Library Catalog

Interactive television; WebTV

Magazines and Newspapers

Use any general, business, or computer database, including

ABI INFORM—*Interactive television*. This is an index to articles in business journals.

ELECTRIC LIBRARY—*Internet and television* (for transcripts of television news shows)

COMPUTER SELECT—*Interactive television; Set-top box*. This database will give you more about how it works and less about why.

PERIODICAL ABSTRACTS

Internet

Try a keyword search for *WebTV* or *Oracle*, the two major players in this technology at the time of this writing.

ProActive's WebTV Resources—www.net4tv.com/proactive/webtvres.htm

Microsoft's *WebCT* page—www.webtv.net. Sections on this site include definitions, what's new, retailers, equipment, and so forth.

Federal Communications Commission—www.fcc.gov. Use the search engine at the FCC site to find federal guidelines.

Antispam on WebCT—vega.webtv.net/antispam. This site provides good information about a potential problem.

Agencies to Contact

WebTV, WeCare@webtv.net, webtv.net

Related Jumpstarts

See Electronic Copyright

94 WELFARE REFORM

Search Terms

Welfare-To-Work

Block Grants

Child Welfare

Poverty and Welfare Reform

Welfare Recipients

Welfare Overhaul Law

Food Stamps

Food for Thought

You will definitely need to refine this large topic. You may just want to report on one of the issues, such as child welfare or the food stamp program.

⌐ How will the Welfare Overhaul Law reduce welfare dependency?

⌐ What is the correlation between welfare and teenage pregnancy? How will the new law address this and other welfare problems?

⌐ Will new laws help or hurt needy children? Legal immigrants? Illegal immigrants?

⌐ If welfare is a generational or an ethnic problem, how does the new law address this problem?

⌐ How can a new law force or encourage or assist welfare recipients to change their lifestyle?

Background and Statistics

Facts on File, "Highlights of the Welfare Overhaul Law." Also use *Facts on File* for updates.

CQ Researcher (online version, *CQ Library,* also available)—*Welfare and Social Services*

Issues & Controversies on File (online version, *Facts.com,* also available)

The Library Catalog

Welfare Reform; Public Welfare, Economic Assistance (Domestic) And Welfare Recipients.

Magazines and Newspapers

Any government, general, or newspaper database will be good, including

Your local newspaper for local concerns.

PERIODICAL ABSTRACTS—*Welfare Overhaul* and *Welfare Reform*

US GOVERNMENT REPORT—Subject tree search—*Domestic Affairs/Social Programs/Welfare.* Gives great background information (before the new law).

WASHINGTON POST—www.washingtonpost.com. Get the *Post's* viewpoint, full-text for the most recent two weeks.

Internet

Thomas—thomas.loc.gov. Do a keyword search on *Welfare Overhaul Law.* Also, use the index for the *Congressional Record* under *welfare overhaul.* This is an actual transcript of congressional meetings.

Megalaw—www.megalaw.com. (to locate laws and cases by state; also includes federal law)

Cornell Law School—www.law.cornell.edu (for state statutes by broad topic or by state)

U.S. Census Bureau—www.census.gov/hhes/www/poverty.html (for poverty statistics, which are essential for proof of need)

Department of Health and Human Services—www.os.dhhs.gov. Get statistics and other information about welfare. Search your local state also.

Welfare Timeline 1932–1996—home.sprynet.com/~keithco/welfare9.htm. Timelines can be very useful to show change.

Agencies to Contact

Try the telephone book for your state department of human services.

AFDC and Food Stamp Programs, 810 First St. N.E., Ste 500, Washington, DC 20002, www.census.gov/socdemo/www/whatAFDC.html

Related Jumpstarts

See Educating Homeless Children; The Homeless; Hunger in America; Social Security Reform

95 → WOMEN'S ATHLETICS

Search Terms

Sports for Women

Sex Discrimination in Sports

Women and Sports

College Sports

Equity and Gender in Sports

Food for Thought

Women's sports are very popular, from ice-skating to basketball (Go Comets!). However, women do not make as much money playing these sports as men do. This is an emotional topic for some. Think about it from the standpoint of college scholarships or professional sports. From your research, create a salary comparison chart. (That will be an eye-opener.) Following are a few ideas for topic refinement:

- Should women's athletic programs receive as much money as men's programs? What is being done to make funding more equitable?

- Should women train the way men do? Why or why not?

- Has participating in team sports traditionally given men a career edge over women?

- Consider the girl's National Soccer Team that has been so successful as a case study.

- Will women's basketball help establish women's sports on television and other media?

Background and Statistics

Congressional Quarterly. Consult the bibliography for additional resources.

CQ Researcher (online version, CQ Library, also available)

The Library Catalog

Women in Sports; Sports for Women; Sports—Women; Women—Athletics

Magazines and Newspapers

Use any general or news database, including the following:

ERIC—www.nhmccd.edu/lrc/kc/eric.html. This education index will be helpful for finding information on athletics programs in high schools and colleges. Try the ERIC digest for full text articles about educational topics.

MEDLINE—igm.nlm.nih.org. Use this medical database if you are interested in the physiological aspects of training for female athletes. Suggested search: *Women and (Sports or Athlet?*

PERIODICAL ABSTRACTS or any general index will find the most articles on this topic.

Internet

Use the Internet to look for specific women athletes or perhaps search for women in the Olympic games or specific sports teams; for example, basketball or soccer.

Women in the Game—www.i-win-.com/secure/statuswinter98/womangame.html

Women's Sports Foundation—www.womenssportsfoundation.org. Includes grants, resources, and equity issues.

Agencies to Contact

Women's Sports Foundation, 800-227-3988, www.lifetimetv.com/WoSport. Provides information on women's sports, physical fitness, and sports medicine.

Related Jumpstarts

See Athletes as Role Models; Fitness for Children; Gender Differences; Sports and Lifelong Benefits

96 → WORK ETHIC

Search Terms

Work and Ethics and (Any Below)

Conduct of Life

Professional Conduct

Performance Standards

Quality of Work Life

Work Motivation

Food for Thought

Work ethic may be defined as one's sense of responsibility and loyalty to a job, identifying the amount of work needed and the accountability of an employee to fill that need. Do Americans still feel a responsibility to give a day's work for a day's pay? Perhaps the creation of huge companies and the lack of a feeling of company loyalty or job security is an emotional factor. Perhaps the fact that people do not expect to stay in one job for a long time contributes to the way they feel about their work. Choose a position on this issue, but be sure to find information on both sides so your argument will have substance.

⌐ What is a "work ethic?" Are work ethics changing? Why or why not?

⌐ How does the concept of a work ethic affect society as a whole?

⌐ Can workplace ethics be taught?

⌐ Does company loyalty (or lack of it) contribute to a poor work ethic?

⌐ Should companies be responsible for improving employee/company loyalty?

Background and Statistics

American Work Values: Their Origin and Development

Taking Sides: Clashing Views on Controversial Issues in Business Ethics and Society

CQ Researcher (online version, *CQ Library*, also available)—*Business and Industry; Business Ethics*

Encyclopedia of Sociology—Work Motivation

Gallup Pole—Ethics or Moral Values

Statistical Abstract of the United States (online version available at www.census.gov /stat_abstract)

Survey of Social Science—Protestant Ethic

The Library Catalog

Work Ethic; Performance Standards

Magazines and Newspapers

Use any business, general, or newspaper index, including

ABI INFORM. Indexes business-related periodicals. This is the best source; its focus is on business.

Newspapers online at www.usanewspapers.com or www.ecola.com/news/press

PERIODICAL ABSTRACTS or another general database is probably your best bet for an English paper. Try *Work Ethic* as a major subject.

Internet

Ethics and Corruption in the Public Sector—www.oecd.org. Use the search engine.

DePaul University Business and Ethics Site—www.depaul.edu/ethics/contents .html (for articles and interesting links)

Agencies to Contact

This is a great topic for a small survey or telephone interviews. Select local companies and ask a few of your questions. Most companies will take time for your questions if you are organized. Get your results and draw conclusions. You might ask questions like the following:

- ⋏ How many employees does your company have?
- ⋏ How long (on average) do employees stay with your company?
- ⋏ What benefits does your company offer employees?
- ⋏ What kind of training do you offer employees? [List them.]
- ⋏ Are there advancement tracks available for your employees? If so, what are they?
- ⋏ List things your company does to retain employees.

Related Jumpstarts

See Drug Testing in the Workplace; Flexible Work Schedules; Sexual Harassment in the Workplace

WORLD POPULATION AND HUNGER

Search Terms

Thomas Malthus

Women and Population

Environment and Population

Sustainable Development and (Population or Hunger)

Third World Countries and (Population or Hunger)

Food for Thought

This is a topic so broad that it can be broken down in many different ways, concerning the effect of population growth on the environment, hunger, religion, or women (birth control). Hunger is a by-product of the problems caused by world population and should be worked into your report, if it interests you. We suggest you pick a small issue for a four-to-five-page paper because there is a great deal of information. Possible interesting broad issues include the following:

⋏ Does population growth continue to widen the gap between the "haves" and "have nots?"

⋏ Should governments limit families in countries where overpopulation is a factor?

⋏ Is religion a major factor in population growth? What role do religious beliefs play?

⋏ Does it infringe on human rights when a society limits family size?

You may find information about food distribution—getting food from the place where it was grown to where it is needed. That is a great economics topic. Many Third World countries have population limitations; you may find that to be an interesting topic.

Background and Statistics

Atlas of World Population History

CQ Researcher (online version, *CQ Library,* also available)—*World Population*

Issues & Controversies on File (online version, *Facts.com,* also available)—*Global Population Growth*

State of the World

World Resources

The Library Catalog

Population; (Country Name)—Population; Birth Control—Population Control

Magazines and Newspapers

Use any general or newspaper database, including

NEWSPAPERS online at www.nhmccd.edu/lrc/kc/subjects.html#news

PERIODICAL ABSTRACTS (for magazine articles)

Internet

World Population Guide—www.nhmccd.edu/lrc/kc/worldpop-assign.html. This is a library guide from Kingwood College.

CIA World Fact Book—www.odci.gov/cia/publications/factbook/index.html. Get statistics by country.

Food and Agriculture Organization—www.fao.org/default.htm. The FAO's mandate is to raise levels of nutrition and standards of living, to improve agricultural productivity, and to improve the condition of rural populations. Great information and links.

Brown University HungerWeb—www.brown.edu/Departments/World_Hunger_Program/index.html. The aim of this site is to help prevent and eradicate hunger by facilitating the free exchange of ideas and information regarding the causes of and solutions to hunger.

Agencies to Contact

World Watch Institute, 1776 Massachusetts Ave. NW, Washington, DC 20037, www.worldwide.org

United Nations Population Fund, 220 E. 42nd St., New York NY 10017, www.unfpa.org

Try the local Salvation Army or online at www.salvationarmyusa.org. Contact your local unit for information about families. This organization has records that will be available to you. Have your questions ready before you call.

Related Jumpstarts

See Abortion; The Homeless; Hunger in America

98 YEAR-ROUND SCHOOLS

Search Terms

Year-Round Schools

Year-Round Education

Extended School Year

Alternative Schedul? and School

Food for Thought

Many school systems have tried year-round school and found that it creates many problems for families. What are some of these problems? How have these problems been solved? School districts around the country have tried it. Are they continuing with this schedule? You may look for a district where this program has been tried and then talk with school officials about its success or lack of success. There will be more information for more recent years.

- ⅄ Does a year-round school schedule cost the school district more money, or does it save money? Is it a more effective use of costly schools? Does it save the cost of erecting additional buildings? Find other arguments for (or against) year-round schools.

- ⅄ What is the effect of year-round schooling on student learning and retention? In what ways does alternative scheduling affect transient students?

- ⅄ How does year-round school scheduling affect family vacations? Scheduling for families with several children? Working parents?

Background and Statistics

CQ Researcher (online version, *CQ Library*, also available)—*Elementary and Secondary Schools*; *Year-Round Schools*

Prisoners of Time: The Report of the National Education Commission on Time and Learning

The Library Catalog

Year Round School; School Year; Education—Schedules

Magazines and Newspapers

Use any education, newspaper, or general database, including

ERIC—www.nhmccd.edu/lrc/kc/eric.html. This is the best source for articles.

Your local newspaper for schools in your area.

Newspapers online at www.ecola.com. This site has both newspapers and journals, separated by subject.

PERIODICAL ABSTRACTS. Use *year round and (schools or education)* for the most comprehensive search. Search multiple years.

Internet

National Association for Year-Round Education—www.NAYRE.org. Provides excellent links for pro-year-round education information. Try to find a balance.

Search year-round school from About.com—about.com (good links and articles).

Department of Education search engine—search.ed.gov. Find information gathered by the Department of Education.

Agencies to Contact

National Association for Year Round Education, PO Box 711386, San Diego, CA 92171-1386, 619-276-5296, info@NAYRE.org, www.nayre.org

Time to Learn, PO Box 12525, Charlotte, NC 28220, 704-525-7151

Related Jumpstarts

See School Choice and Vouchers

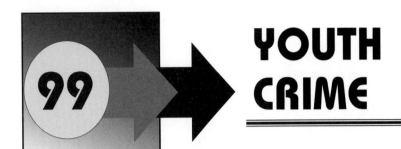

YOUTH CRIME

Search Terms

Crime and Criminals

Criminal Justice

Gangs and (Acceptance or Influence) and Youth

Juvenile Delinquen? (Truncating will pick up *Delinquents* and *Deliquency*)

Youth Crime or Juvenile Crime

Food for Thought

This is a hot topic that was barely an issue 10 years ago. Now, boot camps and teen crime have become the norm, particularly in large cities and suburbs. What is causing this trend? Consider the following:

⅄ Is youth crime on the rise? Are children committing serious crimes at younger ages? Why?

⅄ What social and economic factors may be contributing to this problem?

⅄ Can implementing curfews, treating juvenile offenders as adults, and zero-tolerance policies be effective methods for reducing youth crime? Are there other alternatives?

⅄ Should parents be held criminally responsible for the crimes of their children?

⅄ Are prison boot camps effective in rehabilitating youth?

Background and Statistics

CQ Researcher (online version, *CQ Library*, also available)—*Crime and Criminals*

Crime [Information Plus Series]

Crime and Criminals: Opposing Viewpoints

Encyclopedia of Social Work

Juvenile Crime: Opposing Viewpoints

Sourcebook of Criminal Justice Statistics

Statistical Abstract of the United States

Uniform Crime Reports for the United States (also online at www.fbi.gov/ucr.htm)

Violence: Opposing Viewpoints

The Library Catalog

Youth—Crime; Youth—Drug Use (or Alcohol Use); Dropouts; Juvenile Courts; Juvenile Delinquency; Gangs

Magazines and Newspapers

Any news or general database will be useful, including

ELECTRIC LIBRARY. Provides full-text transcripts from television and radio.

Your local paper (for local crime problems)

Newspapers online at www.usanewspapers.com or www.ecola.com/news/press

PERIODICAL ABSTRACTS. This is probably the best bet for an English paper.

Internet

Crime and Law Enforcement—www.refdesk.com/crime.html

The Bureau of Alcohol, Tobacco and Firearms (ATF)—atf.treas.gov. Use the ATF search engine using *youth crime* for very good articles, lectures, and statistics.

Vision Quest—www.vq.com. Perhaps you have seen on news shows some of the privately owned "camps" that families are sending their troubled children to. You might try to look at several and see what the outcomes are. Are these camps helpful? What kind of research data have been collected to prove this?

Juvenile Boot Camps—www.kci.org. This is a good directory of camps, plus an article on cost and effectiveness.

Youth Crime: Adult Time—law.about.com/newsissues/law/library/weekly/aa103000a.htm (about.com's law issue page)

Related Jumpstarts

See Crime in the Neighborhoods; Gangs; School Violence; Curfews

BIBLIOGRAPHY

Databases Used in This Text

The databases listed below represent what was most widely used by college, school, and public libraries at the time this book went to press. Please be aware, however, that database titles and the media through which they are accessed are subject to extreme changes from year to year.

ABI Inform. An index devoted to business and related topics; contains both full-text entries and abstracts. Available as part of the *ProQuest Database* from Ovid Technologies, 333 Seventh Ave., 4th Floor, New York, NY 10001. (212) 563-3006. Fax (212) 563-3784. E-mail: sales@ovid.com. Also available directly from Bell and Howell Information and Learning (see also *Periodical Abstracts* on page 203).

CINAHL (Cumulative Index of Nursing and Allied Health Literature). An index devoted to the health sciences; provides citations and abstracts to articles. Available from Ovid Technologies, 333 Seventh Ave., 4th Floor, New York, NY 10001. (212) 563-3006. Fax (212) 563-3784. E-mail: sales@ovid.com. Also available from EBSCO (see *EBSCOhost* for complete information).

Computer Select. A full-text index devoted to computers and software. Provides product information and specifications, company profiles, selected Web sites, and articles related to computers. Available from Software Vista, Inc. at (800) 419-0313. E-mail: info@shamancorp.com.

CQ Researcher and *CQ Weekly Report.* Includes the full text of *CQ Researcher*, a weekly in-depth examination of a "hot topic," and *CQ Weekly Report*, a weekly overview of Congress. Available from Congressional Quarterly Customer Service and Order Dept., WEB1, 1414 22nd St. N.W., Washington, DC 20037. (800) 638-1710. E-mail: muarley@cq.com.

EBSCOhost. A full-text general index that links together a host of subject-specific databases. Available from EBSCO Subscription Services, Division Headquarters, PO Box 2543, Birmingham, AL 35202-2543. Division General Manager: (205) 991-6600. 1-800-633-4604. Fax (205) 995-1518. Also on the Web at www.epnet.com.

Electric Library. A full-text general index that covers periodical articles, books, maps, and transcripts of radio and television programs. Available from Infonautics Corporation at (800) 304-3542. Also on the Web at elibrary.com.

ERIC (Education Resource Information Clearinghouse). The most comprehensive index devoted to education-related articles and books; provides abstracts and citations to articles with the option to order full text. Published by the Information Institute of Syracuse University and funded in part by the U.S. Department of Education. Available free in limited form on the Web as *Ask ERIC* at ericir.syr .edu/Eric or as *ERIC Digests* at www.ed.gov/databases/ERIC_Digests/index. Also available in complete form from EBSCO Subscription Services (see *EBSCOhost*) or Ovid Technologies (see *ABI Inform*).

Facts.com. Includes the full texts of *Facts on File World Digest, Reuter News, Issues & Controversies on File, Today's Science, World Almanac,* and *World Almanac Encyclopedia.* Available from Facts on File News Services, 11 Penn Plaza, 15th Floor, New York, NY 10001-2006. (212) 290-8090 or (800) 363-7976. Internet: www.facts.com.

General Science Full Text. Subjects covered include biology, chemistry, astronomy, conservation, earth science, medicine, nutrition, oceanography, and zoology; provides full texts, abstracts, and citations to articles from 191 periodicals. Available from the H. W. Wilson Company, 950 University Ave., Bronx, NY 10452. (800) 367-6770/(718) 588-8400. Internet: www.hwwilson.com/default.cfm.

Health Source Plus. Formerly called *Health Resource Plus.* Provides full texts from over 270 periodicals, 1100 pamphlets, and 20 books; also includes abstracts from some 440 periodicals. Covers nutrition, exercise, medical self-care, drugs and alcohol, plus many more health-related topics. Available from EBSCO Subscription Services. See *EBSCOhost* for subscription information.

Humanities Full Text. Provides full texts and abstracts from 500 English-language periodicals dealing with literature and language, history, philosophy, archaeology, classical studies, folklore, gender studies, performing arts, history, religion, and theology. Available from the H. W. Wilson Company, 950 University Ave., Bronx, NY 10452. (800) 367-6770/(718) 588-8400. Internet: www.hwwilson .com/default.cfm.

InfoTrac (Academic Index or Academic Index ASAP). A general index that provides full texts and abstracts from a huge selection of periodicals. Available from The Gale Group, PO Box 9187, Farmington Hills, MI 48333-9187. (800) 877-GALE (Monday-Friday, 8:00 A.M. to 5 P.M. EST). Fax (800) 414-5043. E-mail: galeord@galegroup.com.

MEDLINE. The National Library of Medicine's premier bibliographic database covering the fields of medicine, nursing, dentistry, veterinary medicine, the health care system, and the pre-clinical sciences. Provides bibliographic citations and author abstracts from more than 4,000 biomedical journals. Available free from PubMed at www.ncbi.nlm.nih.gov/entrez/query.fcgi or igm.nlm.nih.gov.

National Newspaper Index. A full-text index devoted to articles in *The New York Times, Christian Science Monitor, The Washington Post, The Los Angeles Times, and The Wall Street Journal.* Available from The Gale Group, PO Box 9187, Farmington Hills, MI 48333-9187. (800) 877-GALE (Monday-Friday, 8:00 A.M. to 5 P.M. EST). Fax (800) 414-5043. E-mail: galeord@galegroup.com.

New York Times Index. Full-text index to the *The New York Times.* Available as part of a package in the *ProQuest Database* from Bell & Howell Information and Learning (formerly known as UMI), 300 North Zeeb Rd., PO Box 1346, Ann Arbor, MI 48106. (800) 521-0600 or (734) 761-4700. E-mail: info@umi.com.

PaperChase. Online medical database designed for use by both health professionals and the general public; includes MEDLINE, Aidsline, CancerLit, HealthSTAR, OLDMEDLINE, and CINAHL in one index. Provides citations and abstracts with full texts available via fax or mail. Available from PaperChase, 21 Autumn St, 4th Floor, Boston, MA 02215. (800) 722-2075 or (617) 632-0117. Fax (617) 632-0119. E-mail: pch@caregroup.harvard.edu.

Periodical Abstracts. A full-text general index available as part of the *ProQuest Database.* Available from Bell & Howell Information and Learning (formerly known as UMI), 300 North Zeeb Rd., PO Box 1346, Ann Arbor, MI 48106. (800) 521-0600 or (734) 761-4700. E-mail: info@umi.com. Also available from Ovid Technologies (see *ABI Inform*).

SIRS Government Reporter. Provides full texts of current and historic government documents, landmark and recent U.S. Supreme Court decisions, plus facts on federal departments, agencies, and elected leaders. Available from SIRS Mandarin, Inc., PO Box 272348, Boca Raton, FL 33427-2348. (800) 232-7479. Internet: www.sirs.com.

Washington Post Index. Full-text index to *The Washington Post.* Available as part of a package in the *ProQuest Database* from Bell & Howell Information and Learning (formerly known as UMI), 300 North Zeeb Rd., PO Box 1346, Ann Arbor, MI 48106. (800) 521-0600 or (734) 761-4700. E-mail: info@umi.com. Also available from Ovid Technologies (see *ABI Inform*).

WESTLAW. A comprehensive, full-text legal database. Provides information on cases, statutes, public records, and court dockets; legal forms, tax, insurance, and securities resources; and articles from legal periodicals. Available from the West Group at www.westlaw.com/Tours/overview/tnon1.wl.

Print Sources Used in This Text

Please note that because many of the sources included in this bibliography deal with current issues, they are updated regularly. The reader should look for the most recent edition of any title included here. This is true especially of titles in the following series: Information Plus, Opposing Viewpoints, and Taking Sides.

The ABC-CLIO Companion to Women in the Workplace. Schneider, Dorothy, and Carl J. Schneider. Santa Barbara, CA: ABC-CLIO, 1993.

Abortion: An Eternal Social and Moral Issue. Rein, Mei Ling, and Nancy Jacobs, eds. Wylie, TX: Information Plus, published biennially.

Abortion: Decisions of the United States Supreme Court: The 1980's. Harrison, Maureen, and Steve Gilbert, eds. Beverly Hills, CA: Excellent Books, 1993.

Abortion: Opposing Viewpoints. Stephens, Carrie. San Diego: Greenhaven Press, 2000 (updated regularly).

Abortion, Medicine, and the Law. 4th ed., rev. Butler, J. Douglas, and David F. Walbert. New York: Facts on File, 1992.

Academic Crisis of the Community College. McGrath, Dennis, and Martin B. Spear. Albany: State University of New York Press, 1991.

Addiction: Opposing Viewpoints. San Diego: Greenhaven Press, 2000.

Age of Propaganda. Pratkanis, Anthony R., and Elliot Aronson. New York: W. H. Freeman, 2001.

Alcohol: Opposing Viewpoints. San Diego: Greenhaven Press, 1998.

Alcohol and Tobacco. Wylie, TX: Information Plus (published biennially).

Alcohol in Western Society from Antiquity to 1800: A Chronological History. Austin, Gregory et al. Santa Barbara, CA: ABC-CLIO, 1985.

Almanac of American Politics. Barone, Michael, Grant Ujifusa, and Douglas Matthews, comps. Boston: Gambit, 2000 (published biennially).

Almanac of Higher Education. Chicago: University of Chicago Press, 1995.

Almanac of Renewable Energy. Golob, Richard, and Eric Brus. New York: Holt, 1993.

Alternative Fuels and the Environment. Sterrett, Frances S., ed. Boca Raton, FL: Lewis, 1995.

Alternative Healing: The Complete A-Z Guide. Kastner, Mark. New York: Holt, 1996.

Alternative Health and Medicine Encyclopedia. Marti, James. New York: Gale Research, 1997.

America Beyond 2001: Opposing Viewpoints. Markley, Oliver, and Walter R. McCuan, eds. San Diego: Greenhaven Press, 1996 (updated regularly).

American Cancer Society's Guide to Complementary and Alternative Cancer Methods. Atlanta: American Cancer Society, 2000.

American Family. Wylie, TX: Information Plus (published biennially).

American Heritage Dictionary of the English Language. Boston: Houghton Mifflin, 2000.

American Homelessness: A Reference Handbook. Hombs, Mary Ellen. Contemporary World Issues. Santa Barbara, CA: ABC-CLIO, 1994.

American Manhood: Transformations in Masculinity from the Revolution to the Modern Era. Rotondo, Anthony E. New York: Basic Books, 1993.

American Prison System: The Reference Shelf. New York: H. W. Wilson, 2001.

American Sport Culture: The Humanistic Dimensions. Umphlett, Wiley Lee, ed. Lewisburg, PA: Bucknell University Press, 1985.

American Values: Opposing Viewpoints. Hurley, Jennifer A., ed. San Diego: Greenhaven Press, 2001.

American Work Values: Their Origin and Development. Bernstein, Paul. Albany: State University of New York Press, 1997.

America's International Trade: A Reference Handbook. Miller, E. Willard, and Ruby M. Miller. Santa Barbara, CA: ABC-CLIO, 1995.

Animal Experimentation. Haugen, David M., ed. San Diego: Greenhaven Press, 2000.

Animal Rights: A Reference Handbook. Sherry, Clifford J. Contemporary World Issues. Santa Barbara, CA: ABC-CLIO, 1994.

Animal Rights: Opposing Viewpoints. San Diego: Greenhaven Press, 1999.

Atlas of the Holocaust. Gilbert, Martin. New York: William Morrow, 1993.

Atlas of World Population History. McEvedy, Colin. New York: Facts on File, 1979.

Biographical Dictionary of American Cult and Sect Leaders. Melton, J. Gordon. New York: Garland, 1986.

Biomedical Ethics: Opposing Viewpoints. Roleff, Tamara L., ed. San Diego: Greenhaven Press, 1998.

Book of the States. Council of State Government, and American Legislators' Association. Lexington, KY: Council of State Governments (published biennially).

By the Sweat and Toil of Children. Bureau of International Labor Affairs. U.S. Department of Labor. Washington, DC: The Bureau, 1994–1995.

Campaign and Election Reform. Utter, Glen H., and Ruth Ann Strickland. Santa Barbara, CA: ABC-CLIO, 1997.

Campaign Finance: The Reference Shelf. New York: H. W. Wilson, 2001.

Capital Punishment. Wylie, TX: Information Plus (published biennially).

Capital Punishment: A Reference Handbook. Kronenwitten, Michael. Santa Barbara, CA: ABC-CLIO, 1993.

Child Labor Is Not Cheap: A Unit for Grades 8–12 and Adults. Sanders, Amy. Minneapolis, MN: Resource Center of the Americas, 1997.

Cities of the United States. Detroit: Gale Research, 1998 (updated periodically).

Columbia University College of Physicians and Surgeons Complete Home Guide to Mental Health. 3rd rev. ed. Tapley, Donald F. et al, eds. New York: Crown, 1995.

Coming Plague: Newly Emerging Diseases in a World Out of Balance. New York: Farrar, Straus and Giroux, 1994.

The Company We Keep. Roueche, John, Lynn Sullivan Tabor, and Suzanne D. Roueche. Washington, DC: Community College Press, 1995.

Complete History of the Death Penalty. Mitchell, Hayley R. San Diego: Greenhaven Press, 2001.

Complete Idiot's Guide to Surfing the Internet with WebTV. Indianapolis: Que, 1999.

Congressional Quarterly Almanac. Washington, DC: Congressional Quarterly News Features, 1999 (updated annually).

Conservation and Environmentalism: An Encyclopedia. Paehlke, Robert, ed. New York: Garland, 1995.

Contagious and Non-Contagious Diseases Sourcebook. Detroit: Omnigraphics, 1996.

The Copyright Handbook: How to Protect and Use Written Works. 5th ed. Fishman, Stephen. Berkeley, CA: Nolo Press, 2000.

The Copyright Primer for Librarians and Educators. 2d ed. Bruwelheide, Janis H. Chicago: American Library Association, 1995.

CQ Researcher. Washington, D C: Congressional Quarterly in conjunction with EBSCO, 1991– (updated weekly). Also available online at library.cqpress.com.

CQ Weekly. Washington, DC: Congressional Quarterly, 1998– (weekly journal). Also available online at library.cqpress.com.

Credit Cards and the Law. Fowler, Mavis. Dobbs Ferry, NY: Oceana, 1995.

Crime. Wylie, TX: Information Plus (published biennially).

Crime and Criminals: Opposing Viewpoints. San Diego: Greenhaven Press, 2000 (updated regularly).

Culture Wars: Opposing Viewpoints. San Diego: Greenhaven Press, 1999 (updated regularly).

Current Issues and Enduring Questions: A Guide to Critical Thinking and Argument, with Readings. 5th ed. Barnet, Sylvan and Hugo Bedaw, eds. Boston: Bedford, 1999 (updated regularly).

Death and Dying: Opposing Viewpoints. San Diego: Greenhaven Press, 1999 (updated regularly).

Death and Dying: Who Decides? Rein, Meiling, Abbey M. Begun, and Jacquelyn F. Quiram, eds. Wylie, TX: Information Plus, published biennially.

Diagnostic and Statistical Manual of Mental Disorders: DSM-IV, 4th ed. American Psychological Association. Washington, DC: American Psychological Association, 1994.

Diagnostic and Statistical Manual of Mental Disorders: DSM-IV-TR. 4th ed., text revision. American Psychological Association. Washington, DC: American Psychological Association, 2000.

Digest of Education Statistics. National Center for Education Statistics, Office of Educational Research, and Improvement Center for Education Statistics. Washington, DC: U. S. Department of Health, Education and Welfare, Education Division, National Center for Education Statistics, 1995– (updated annually).

Domestic Violence: A Reference Handbook. McCue, Margi Laird. Santa Barbara, CA: ABC-CLIO, 1995.

Drug Abuse: Opposing Viewpoints. Torr, James D., ed. San Diego: Greenhaven Press, 1999 (updated regularly).

Drug Testing: Issues and Options. New York: Oxford University Press, 1991.

Drugs, Drug Testing, and You. Clayton, Lawrence. New York: Rosen, 1997.

Drugs Workplace Testing (video). National Institute of Justice. Rockville, MD: National Institute of Justice, 1990.

Drunk Driving Law. Jasper, Margaret C. Dobbs Ferry, NY: Oceana, 1999.

Eating Disorders: A Reference Sourcebook. Lemberg, Raymond, ed. Phoenix: Oryx Press, 1999.

Eating Disorders: Opposing Viewpoints. San Diego: Greenhaven Press, 2001.

Education. Wylie, TX: Information Plus (published biennially).

Education: Opposing Viewpoints. San Diego: Greenhaven Press, 2000 (updated regularly).

Education Sourcebook: Basic Information About National Expectations and Goals. Gough, Jeanne, ed. Detroit: Omnigraphics, 1997.

Encyclopedia of Aging: A Comprehensive Resource in Gerontology and Geriatrics. Maddox, George L., ed. New York: Springer, 2001.

Encyclopedia of American Education. Unger, Harlow G., ed. New York: Facts on File, 2001.

Encyclopedia of Banking & Finance. Woelfel, Charles J., ed. Chicago: Probus, 1994.

Encyclopedia of Bioethics. Reich, Warren T., ed. New York: Macmillan, 1995.

Encyclopedia of Career Change and Work Issues. Jones, Lawrence K., ed. Phoenix: Oryx Press, 1992.

The Encyclopedia of Climate and Weather. Schneider, Stephen H., ed. New York: Oxford University Press, 1996.

Encyclopedia of Crime and Justice. Kadish, Sanford H., ed. New York: Free Press, 1983.

Encyclopedia of Criminology and Deviant Behavior. Bryant, Clifton D., ed. Philadelphia: Brunner Routledge, 2000.

Encyclopedia of Drugs, Alcohol, and Addictive Behavior. Carson-Dewitt, Rosalyn, ed. New York: Macmillan, 2000.

Encyclopedia of Educational Research. 6th ed. Alkin, Marvin C., ed. New York: Macmillan, 1992.

Encyclopedia of Genocide. Charny, Israel, ed. Santa Barbara, CA: ABC-CLIO, 1999.

The Encyclopedia of Homosexuality. Dynes, Wayne R., ed. New York: Garland, 1990.

Encyclopedia of Management. 4th ed. Helms, Marilyn, ed. Detroit: Gale Group, 2000.

Encyclopedia of Marriage and the Family. Levinson, David, ed. New York: Macmillan, 1995.

Encyclopedia of New Age Beliefs. Ankerberg, John, and John Weldon. Eugene, OR: Harvest House, 1996.

The Encyclopedia of Nutrition and Good Health. Ronzio, Robert A. New York: Facts on File, 1997.

Encyclopedia of Psychology. Kazdin, Alan E., ed. Washington, DC: American Psychological Association, 2000.

Encyclopedia of Social Work. National Association of Social Workers. New York: National Association of Social Workers, 1995.

Encyclopedia of Sociology. Borgatta, Edgar F., ed. New York: Macmillan, 2000.

Encyclopedia of Special Education: A Reference Handbook for the Education of the Handicapped and Other Exceptional Children and Adults. Reynolds, Cecil R., and Elaine Fletcher-Janzen, eds. New York: John Wiley, 1999.

The Encyclopedia of Suicide. Evanson, Glen, and Norman L. Farberow. New York: Facts on File, 1988.

Encyclopedia of the Environment. Kellert, Stephen, ed. New York: Franklin Watts, 1999.

The Encyclopedia of the United States Congress. Bacon, Donald C., Roger H. Davidson, and Morton Keller, eds. New York: Simon & Schuster, 1995.

Encyclopedic Handbook of Cults in America. Melton, J. Gordon. New York: Garland, 1992.

Energy. Wylie, TX: Information Plus (published biennially).

Energy Handbook. 2d ed. Loftness, Robert L. New York: Van Nostrand Reinhold, 1984.

The Environment. Wylie, TX: Information Plus (published biennially).

Environmental Almanac. Hoyle, Russ, ed. Detroit: Gale Research, 1993.

Epidemics: Opposing Viewpoints. San Diego: Greenhaven Press, 1999.

Ethical and Legal Aspects of Nursing. 2d ed. Catalano, Joseph T. Springhouse, PA: Springhouse, 1995.

Euthanasia: A Reference Handbook. Roberts, Carol S., and Martha Gorman. Santa Barbara, CA: ABC-CLIO, 1996.

Euthanasia: Opposing Viewpoints. Williams, Mary E., ed. San Diego: Greenhaven Press, 2000 (updated regularly).

Extremist Groups: Opposing Viewpoints. San Diego: Greenhaven Press, 2001.

Facts on File. New York: Facts on File, 1963– (published weekly).

Family: Opposing Viewpoints. San Diego: Greenhaven Press, 1999 (updated regularly).

Feminism: Opposing Viewpoints. Hurley, Jennifer A., ed. San Diego: Greenhaven Press, 2001.

Focus on Eating Disorders: A Reference Handbook. O'Halloran, M. Sean. Santa Barbara, CA: ABC-CLIO, 1993.

Food and Animal Borne Diseases Sourcebook. Bellenir, Karen, and Peter D. Dresser, eds. Detroit: Omnigraphics, 1995.

Future of the Interactive Television Services Marketplace: What Should Consumers Expect? Washington, DC: US GPO, 2001. Also available online at purl.access.gpo.gov/GPO/LPS10574.

Gale Encyclopedia of Science. McGrath, Kimberly, ed. Detroit: Gale Group, 2001.

The Gallup Poll: Public Opinion. Gallup, George Horace. Wilmington, DE: Scholarly Resources, 1978– (updated annually).

Gambling. Wylie, TX: Information Plus, published biennially.

Gangs: Opposing Viewpoints. Egendorf, Laura K., ed. San Diego: Greenhaven Press, 2001 (updated regularly).

Garbage. Wylie, TX: Information Plus (published biennially).

Genes. Lewin, Benjamin. New York: John Wiley, 1987.

Genetic Engineering: Opposing Viewpoints. Torr, James D., ed. San Diego: Greenhaven Press, 2000 (updated regularly).

Government Assistance Almanac. Dumouchel, J. Robert. Washington, DC: Foggy Bottom, 1985– (updated annually).

Great Cases in Constitutional Law. George, Robert P. Princeton, NJ: Princeton University Press, 2000.

The Greening of American Business. Sullivan, Thomas F. P., ed. Rockville, MD: Government Institutes, 1992.

Growing Old in America. Wylie, TX: Information Plus (published biennially).

Growing Up in America. Wylie, TX: Information Plus (published biennially).

Growing Up in Twentieth Century America: A History and Reference Guide. West, Elliott. Westport, CT: Greenwood, 1996.

The Guide to American Law Yearbook: Everyone's Legal Encyclopedia. St. Paul, MN: West, 1990.

Gun Control. Wylie, TX: Information Plus (published biennially).

Handbook of Child Psychology. 5th ed. Damon, William. New York: John Wiley, 1998.

Handbook of U.S. Labor Statistics: Employment, Earnings, Prices, Productivity, and Other Labor Data. Lanham, MD: Bernan Press (published annually).

Health: A Concern for Every American. Wylie, TX: Information Plus (published biennially).

Health Care: Opposing Viewpoints. Torr, James D., ed. San Diego: Greenhaven Press, 2000 (updated regularly).

Healthy People 2000: Midcourse Review and 1995 Revisions. U.S. Department of Health and Human Services, Public Health Service, Health Resources and Services Administration, Maternal and Child Health Bureau. Washington, DC: U.S. Department of Health and Human Services, 1995.

Healthy People 2000: National Health Promotion and Disease Prevention Objectives Related to Mothers, Infants, Children, Adolescents, and Youth. U.S. Department of Health and Human Services, Public Health Service, Health Resources and Services Administration, Maternal and Child Health Bureau. Boston: Jones and Bartlett, 1992.

Historic Documents. Congressional Quarterly, Inc. Washington, DC: Congressional Quarterly, 1945– (updated annually).

Homeless Children and Youth: A New American Dilemma. Kryder-Coe, Julee, Lester M. Salamon, and Janice M. Molnar, eds. New Brunswick, NJ: Transaction, 1991.

Homeless in America. Wylie, TX: Information Plus (published biennially).

Homelessness: A Sourcebook. Fantasia, Rick, and Maurice Isserman. New York: Facts on File, 1994.

Homosexuality: Opposing Viewpoints. Williams, Mary E., ed. San Diego: Greenhaven Press, 1999 (updated regularly).

Hot Zone. Preston, Richard. New York: Random House, 1994.

Human Rights: A Reference Handbook. Redman, Nina, and Lucille Whalen. Santa Barbara, CA: ABC-CLIO, 1998.

Human Rights: Opposing Viewpoints. San Diego: Greenhaven Press, 1998 (updated regularly).

Illegal Drugs. Wylie, TX: Information Plus (published biennially).

Illiberal Education: The Politics of Race and Sex on Campus. D'Souza, Dinesh. New York: Free Press, 1991.

Immigration: Opposing Viewpoints. San Diego: Greenhaven Press, 1998 (updated regularly).

Immigration and Illegal Aliens. Wylie, TX: Information Plus (published biennially).

Inequality: Opposing Viewpoints in Social Problems. San Diego: Greenhaven Press, 1998 (updated regularly).

Injury Facts. National Safety Council, National Safety Council Statistics Division. Chicago: National Safety Council, 1996.

Interracial America: Opposing Viewpoints. San Diego: Greenhaven Press, 2001.

Into the Third Century: A Profile of America. Jacobs, Nancy R., Mark A. Siegel, and Carol D. Foster. Wylie, TX: Information Plus (published biennially).

Introducing WebTV. Freeze, Jill T., and Wayne S. Freeze. Redmond, WA: Microsoft Press, 1998.

Issues & Controversies on File. New York: Facts on File, 1995– (updated weekly).

John T. Malloy's [i.e., Molloy's] New Dress for Success. Molloy, John T. New York: Warner, 1995.

Kiss, Bow and Shake Hands. Morrison, Terri. Holbrook, MA: B. Adams, 1994.

Land and the City: Patterns and Processes of Urban Change. Kivell, Philip. London: Routledge, 1993.

The Legal Rights of Women: Legal Subjects That Most Affect the Lives of Women. Cornblum, Bruce. San Diego: Women's Research, 1995.

Legalized Gambling: A Reference Handbook. Thompson, William Norman. Contemporary World Issues Series. Santa Barbara, CA: ABC-CLIO, 1997.

Lessons of the Locker Room: The Myth of School Sports. Miracle, Andrew W., Jr. and C. Roger Rees. Amherst, NY: Prometheus Books, 1994.

Library in a Book: Eating Disorders. Mathews, John R. New York: Facts on File, 1991.

Macmillan Health Encyclopedia. New York: Macmillan, 1999.

Magill's Survey of Science: Life Sciences Series. Magill, Frank N., ed. Pasadena, CA: Salem Press, 1991.

Male Female Roles: Opposing Viewpoints. San Diego: Greenhaven Press, 2000 (updated regularly).

Marriage, Family and Relationships: A Cross-Cultural Encyclopedia. Broude, Gwen J. Santa Barbara, CA: ABC-CLIO, 1994.

Mass Media: Opposing Viewpoints. San Diego: Greenhaven Press, 1999 (updated regularly).

A Matter of Fact: A Digest of Current Facts, with Citations to Sources. Ann Arbor, MI: Pierian Press (published biannually).

Media Violence: Opposing Viewpoints. San Diego: Greenhaven Press, 1999 (updated regularly).

Mental Measurements Yearbook. Buros Institute of Mental Measurements. Highland Park, NJ: The Mental Measurements Yearbook, 1945– (updated annually).

Minorities: A Changing Role in American Society. Wylie, TX: Information Plus, 2000 (updated regularly).

Multiculturalism in Academe: A Source Book. Morris, Libby V. New York: Garland, 1996.

National Gangs Resource Book: An Encyclopedia Reference. Knox, George W. Bristol, IN: Wyndham Hall Press, 1994.

National Survey of State Laws. Leiter, Richard A. Detroit: Gale Group, 2000.

New Age Encyclopedia. Melton, J. Gordon. Detroit: Gale Research, 1990.

New Women's Dress for Success Book. Molloy, John T. New York: Warner, 1996.

Nurse's Handbook of Law & Ethics. Springhouse, PA: Springhouse, 1992.

Nurse's Legal Handbook. 4th ed. Springhouse, PA: Springhouse, 2000.

Nutrition. Wylie, TX: Information Plus (published biennially).

Occupational Outlook Handbook. U.S. Department of Labor, Bureau of Labor Statistics. Washington, DC: The Bureau, 1998–1999 (published annually). Available online at stats.bls.gov/ocohome.htm.

The Official Guide to American Attitudes: Who Thinks What About the Issues That Shape Our Lives. Mitchell, Susan. Ithaca, NY: New Strategist, 1996.

The Official Guide to the American Marketplace: The Real Facts about How Rich, Well-educated, Healthy, Family-oriented, Hard-working, and Diverse We Are. Russell, Cheryl. Ithaca, NY: New Strategist, 1997.

Organ Transplants. Kittredge, Mary. Philadelphia: Chelsea, 2000.

Oxford Companion to the Mind. Gregory, Richard L., ed. Oxford: Oxford University Press, 1998.

Pay Dirt: The Business of Professional Team Sports. Quirk, James P., and Rodney D. Fort. Princeton, NJ: Princeton University Press, 1997.

The People, the Press, and Politics. Ornstein, Norman, Andrew Kohut, and Larry McCarthy. Reading, MA: Addison-Wesley, 1988.

Physician-Assisted Suicide and Euthanasia. Yount, Lisa. New York: Facts on File, 2000.

Police Brutality: A National Debate. Borstein, Jerry. Hillside, NJ: Enslow, 1993.

Police Brutality: Opposing Viewpoints. Cothran, Helen, ed. San Diego: Greenhaven Press, 2001.

Political Scandals: Opposing Viewpoints. Dudley, William, ed. San Diego: Greenhaven Press, 2001.

Politics in America: Opposing Viewpoints. Tipp, Stacey L., and Carol Wekesser, eds. San Diego: Greenhaven Press, 1992 (updated regularly).

Pollution: Opposing Viewpoints. San Diego: Greenhaven Press, 2000 (updated regularly).

Population History and the Family: A Journal of Interdisciplinary History Reader. Rotberg, Robert I., ed. Cambridge, MA: MIT Press, 2001.

PR: How the Public Relations Industry Writes the News. Blyskal, Jef. New York: William Morrow, 1985

Prisoners of Time: Report of the National Education Commission on Time and Learning. National Education Commission on Time and Learning. Washington, DC: The Commission, 1994.

Prisons and Jails. Wylie, TX: Information Plus (published biennially).

Profile of the Nation. Wylie, TX: Information Plus (published biennially).

Public Schooling in America: A Reference Handbook. Van Scotter, Richard D. Santa Barbara, CA: ABC-CLIO, 1991.

Rape in America: A Reference Handbook. Hall, Rob. Santa Barbara, CA: ABC-CLIO, 1995.

Recycling in America: A Reference Handbook. Strong, Debra L. Santa Barbara, CA: ABC-CLIO, 1997.

Reducing the Health Consequences of Smoking: 25 Years of Progress. U.S. Department of Health and Human Services. Washington, DC: US GPO, 1989.

Regulating Tobacco. Rabin, Robert L., and Stephen D. Sugerman, eds. New York: Oxford University Press, 2001.

Renewable Energy: Sources for Fuels and Electricity. Johansson, Thomas B. et al, eds. Washington, DC: Island Press, 1993.

Riding the Iron Rooster. Theroux, Paul. New York: Putnams, 1988.

The Rights of Lesbians and Gay Men: The Basic ACLU Guide to a Gay Person's Rights. 3d ed. Hunter, Nan D., Sherryl E. Michaelson, and Thomas B. Stoddard. Carbondale, IL: Southern Illinois University Press, 1992.

Road Rage: Causes and Dangers of Aggressive Driving: Hearing Before the Subcommittee on Surface Transportation of the Committee on Transportation and Infrastructure, House of Representatives, One Hundred Fifth Congress, First Session, July 17, 1997. Washington, DC: Government Printing Office, 1997.

Road Rage and Aggressive Driving: Steering Clear of Highway Warfare. James, Leon, and Diane Nahl. Amherst, NY: Prometheus, 2000.

The Rope, the Chair, and the Needle: Capital Punishment in Texas, 1923–1990. Marquart, James W. Austin: University of Texas Press, 1994.

Same Sex Marriage: Pros and Cons: A Reader. Sullivan, Andrew. New York: Vintage Books, 1997.

School Prayer: The Court, the Congress, and the First Amendment. Alley, Robert S. Buffalo, NY: Prometheus Books, 1994.

School Violence. Grapes, Bryan J., ed. San Diego: Greenhaven Press, 2000.

School Violence: A Reference Handbook. Kopka, Deborah L. Santa Barbara, CA: ABC-CLIO, 1997.

School Violence: The Reference Shelf. Bonilla, Denise M. New York: H. W. Wilson, 2000.

Shadow: Five Presidents and the Legacy of Watergate. Woodard, Bob. New York: Simon & Schuster, 1999.

Silent Spring. Carson, Rachel. Boston: Houghton Mifflin, 1987.

Social Significance of Sport: An Introduction to the Sociology of Sport. McPherson, Barry D., James E. Curtis, and John W. Loy. Champaign, IL: Human Kinetics Books, 1989.

Social Welfare. Wylie, TX: Information Plus (published biennially).

Sourcebook of Criminal Justice Statistics. Washington, DC: U.S. Department of Justice, Bureau of Justice Statistics (published annually).

Sport in Society: Issues and Controversies. 7th ed. Coakley, Jay. Boston: McGraw-Hill, 2001.

Sports and Athletes: Opposing Viewpoints. Egandorf, Laura K., ed. San Diego: Greenhaven Press, 1999 (updated regularly).

Sports Ethics: A Handbook. Berlow, Lawrence H. Santa Barbara, CA: ABC-CLIO, 1994.

Sports in America: The Reference Shelf. New York: H. W. Wilson, 2001.

Sports in the Lives of Children and Adolescents: Success on the Field and in Life. Griffin, Robert S. Westport, CT: Praeger, 1998.

Sports Stars. Pare, Michael A. Detroit: UXL (published annually).

Standard Handbook of Hazardous Waste Treatment and Disposal. Freeman, Harry M., ed. New York: McGraw-Hill, 1998.

The State of America's Children Yearbook. Children's Defense Fund. Washington, DC: Children's Defense Fund (published annually).

State of the World: A Worldwatch Institute Report on Progress Toward a Sustainable Society. New York: Norton (published annually).

Statistical Abstract of the United States. U. S. Department of Commerce, Bureau of the Census. Washington, DC: U. S. Department of Commerce, Bureau of the Census, 1878– (published annually). Online version available at www.census.gov/stat_abstract.

Statistical Handbook on Adolescents in America. Chadwick, Bruce A., and Tim B. Heaton, eds. Phoenix: Oryx Press, 1996.

Statistical Handbook on the American Family. Chadwick, Bruce A., and Tim B. Heaton, eds. Phoenix: Oryx Press, 1999.

Statistical Handbook on Violence in America. Dobrin, Adam et. al. Phoenix: Oryx Press, 1996.

Statistical Handbook on Women in America. 2d ed. Taeuber, Cynthia M, comp. and ed. Phoenix: Oryx Press, 1996.

Statistical Record of Children. Schmittroth, Linda, ed. Detroit: Gale Research, 1994.

Statistical Record of Health and Medicine. Dorgan, Charity Anne, ed. Detroit: Gale Research, 1995–1998.

Statistical Record of the Environment. Darnay, Arsen J. Detroit: Gale Research, 1997.

Street Gang Awareness: A Resource Guide for Parents and Professionals. Sachs, Steven L. Minneapolis, MN: Fairview Press, 1997.

Substance Abuse Sourcebook. Bellenir, Karen, ed. Detroit: Omnigraphics, 1996.

Suicide: Opposing Viewpoints. Roleff, Tamara J., ed. San Diego: Greenhaven Press, 1998 (updated regularly).

Survey of Social Science: Sociology Series. Magill, Frank N., ed. Pasadena, CA: Salem Press, 1994.

Taking Sides: Clashing Views on Controversial Issues in Business, Ethics, and Society. 3d ed. Newton, Lisa H., and Maureen M. Ford, eds. Guilford, CT: Dushkin, 1994 (updated regularly).

Teen Legal Rights. Hempelman, Kathleen A. Westport, CT: Greenwood Press, 2000.

Teenage Sexuality: Opposing Viewpoints. Roloff, Tamara L. San Diego: Greenhaven Press, 2001.

Terminal Illness: Opposing Viewpoints. Williams, Mary E. San Diego: Greenhaven Press, 2001 (updated regularly).

Texas Drunk Driving Law. 4th ed. Trichter, J. Gary, and W. Troy McKinney. Charlottesville, VA: Lexis, 2000.

Texas Environmental Almanac. Texas Center for Policy Studies. Austin, TX: University of Texas Press, 2000.

Tobacco and Smoking: Opposing Viewpoints. San Diego: Greenhaven Press, 1998 (updated regularly).

Trends in the Well-Being of America's Children and Youth. U.S. Department of Health and Human Services, Office of the Assistant Secretary for Planning and Evaluation. Washington, DC: U.S. Department of Health and Human Services, Office of the Assistant Secretary for Planning and Evaluation, 1996.

Uniform Crime Reports for the United States. U.S. Federal Bureau of Investigation. Washington, DC: Federal Bureau of Investigation, 1930– (published with varying frequency).

United States Energy Atlas. Cuff, David J. New York: Macmillan, 1986.

Value Line Investment Survey. New York: Value Line, 1995.

Vernon's Texas Statutes and Codes. St. Paul, MN: West, 1990– (published annually).

Violent Relationships. Wylie, TX: Information Plus (published biennially).

The War on Drugs: Opposing Viewpoints. San Diego: Greenhaven Press, 1998 (updated regularly).

The Weather Almanac. Wood, Richard A., ed. Detroit: Gale Research, 1974– (published annually).

West's Encyclopedia of American Law. St. Paul, MN: West, 1999.

Widening Circle of Genocide. Charney, Israel W., ed. New Brunswick, NJ: Transaction, 1994.

Women's Changing Role. Wylie, TX: Information Plus (published biennially).

Women's Rights on Trial: 101 Historic Trials from Anne Hutchinson to the Virginia Military Institute Cadets. Frost-Knappman, Elizabeth, and Kathryn Cullen-DuPont. Detroit: Gale Research, 1997.

Working Women: Opposing Viewpoints. San Diego: Greenhaven Press, 1998 (updated regularly).

World Resources. New York: Basic Books (published biennially).

Year Book of Infectious Disease. Chicago: Year Book Medical (published annually).

Your Rights in the Workplace. 5th ed. Repa, Barbara Kate. Berkeley, CA: Nolo.com, 2000.

SUBJECT DIRECTORY

INDEX

6540